The Teachable Heart
A Six-Month Devotional

Volume 4

David E. Vitt

INTRODUCTION

Welcome to *The Teachable Heart!* My hope is that you have already read *Volumes 1, 2 and 3*, and found enough insight and encouragement within those pages to warrant picking up *Volume 4.*

However, if you're new to *The Teachable Heart* family – welcome aboard! Unlike many devotionals, you'll notice that this one does not follow the calendar. There will not be a hard New Year's Day start date or special messages on Valentine's Day, Mother's Day, or Father's Day. This was quite intentional, so that readers can pick up the book on any day of the week or year without feeling "behind schedule." (Don't we all have enough pressure already?)

If you benefit from the devotions within these pages, please visit *The Teachable Heart* Facebook page or our website where you can find new, daily messages. Just visit: https://theteachableheart.com/classrooms-%26-devotions for more information, or to sign up to receive daily devotions via email.

Don't forget to recommend *The Teachable Heart* to your friends – remember, short devotional books make great gifts too! Lastly, if you liked the book, I'd be honored if you wrote a review on Amazon.com!

May The Greatest Teacher of all help you to learn and grow in your love and knowledge of Him as you read!

Sincerely,

Dave

DEDICATION

Volume 4 was compiled in large part as a birthday gift to my father, Greg Vitt. Dad, I am forever grateful for the times I "caught" you sitting in your favorite chair reading Scripture. If I had a dime for every time I heard you say, "The Bible hasn't lied to me yet," I'd be a rich man! As it is, I received a treasure more valuable than anything this world has to offer – a love of, and respect for, God's Word. Who knew that all these years later, you would become one of *The Teachable Heart's* greatest fans, and my greatest encourager. Don't think your consistent prompts to "keep writing," fell on deaf ears! Love you much – Dave

ACKNOWLEDGEMENTS

I'd again like to thank my wife, Davina, and our daughters, Amanda and Amy, for their ongoing encouragement and support. They fill my world with a great deal of joy and are the willing subjects of many stories!

Special thanks go to my daughter, Amanda, for again lending her critical eye and excellent editing skills to the manuscript. Trust me, she saved you from reading a ton of errors!   Credit for the attractive design of the front and back covers again go to my neighbor and friend JD Fleming – thank you for your dedication to excellence!

Lastly, I'd like to thank Jesus – in Him we have someone worth both reading and writing about. My prayer is that the Lord will take the words on these pages and use them to accomplish His will within your life!

Keep the Heart Teachable,

Dave

A NOTE FOR THOSE WHO RECEIVED THIS BOOK AS A GIFT

First, congratulations! Although a book may not have been your first choice for a gift, at least somebody cares about you! If you are already a follower of Christ, and want to grow in your relationship with Him, this book was written specifically with you in mind! If that does not describe you, don't worry, and don't throw this book out – there is still something of value for you no matter what.

If you were given this book during a time of deep personal struggle or loss, please know that you're not alone and that there is **help for the hurting!** If life has brought you to the edge of your ability to cope, please reach out for help! It IS available, no matter how desperate your situation currently appears. However, this book may not meet that immediate need. <u>If you are in acute emotional distress – severely depressed or suicidal – please call</u>: the Suicide Hotline at **800-273-8255**. Someone is available to speak with you 24/7. If your situation is less desperate, but you would like some trustworthy support and counseling, please contact the American Academy of Christian Counselors at: **800-526-8673;** or visit their site at: <u>www.aacc.net</u>.   They can provide contact information for a counselor in your area.

Finally, if none of the above applies to you, yet you have a sense within your heart that life is passing you by, and something is missing, then please consider the words of Augustine who wrote, "Thou hast made us for Thyself, O Lord, and our heart is restless until it finds its rest in thee."

Friend, the person who gave you this book wants you to find rest for your heart and satisfaction for your soul. Since we were all made by a loving Father in Heaven, that rest is only possible when we are in right, peaceful relationship with Him. Thankfully, God has made a way for that to become your reality by accepting His forgiveness and placing personal faith in His Son, Jesus Christ.

While there is not a "recipe" to follow, there is a need for each person to <u>Admit</u> that they have sinned and fallen short of God's perfect standard. They are to <u>Believe</u> that Christ lived a perfect life, and died on a cross in their place for the forgiveness of that sin. Finally, each person must <u>Choose</u> whether they will accept that gift of grace or not.

If you have questions about any of the above, please reach out to a Bible-believing pastor in your area, or the person who gave you this book. Remember, they care!

FOREWORD

Christian devotions can be defined as quiet times of reflection where believers in Jesus set their minds on the person of Christ in study, prayer, and worship with a desire to become more intimate with Him.

For nearly twenty years Dave Vitt has been assisting believers in the task of becoming more intimate with the Lord Jesus by taking them to the Scriptures to behold and apply the truths of God's Word to their daily walk. The book you are holding in your hands is a compilation of some of his favorite writings. Dave has a unique gift to be able to draw out the depth of the Scriptures in personal, applicable ways that go right to the heart of every-day life. Those of us who are privileged to regularly enjoy Dave's teaching at church have been able to benefit from his keen insight and extensive study. In his devotional writings, Dave gives some of the same wisdom in "bite-sized" chunks in order to bring encouragement and edification to God's people. His ministry is called "The Teachable Heart" because that is what he diligently works to cultivate in himself and desires to see in others. Every day, many people look on-line to "The Teachable Heart" for words of hope from God's Word. Now, in this book, these insights will be available in a more permanent form to a wider audience.

Dave has been a student of Scripture for a long time, as well as a Bible teacher and author. I can say from first-hand experience that he does indeed have a teachable heart. Much of his insight has come through the struggles of applying God's truths to family life and business in the midst of the struggles that are common to all of us. There is a genuineness and warmth to his writing that comes from the knowledge that he is merely a fellow pilgrim on the journey.

Though I am technically Dave's pastor, it has been my great privilege to serve alongside him as a fellow elder in our church. I also sit under his teaching every week in our mid-week Bible study. But the greatest privilege is to be able to call him my friend.
I have no doubt that you, dear reader, will benefit from the insights found in this book. I am excited for you. It's my sincere prayer that you will find encouragement every day as you set your heart to have a more intimate walk with the Savior.

May we all constantly desire and cultivate a teachable heart.

Pastor Keith Gibson

DAY 1 – REQUIREMENTS

It's the first message of a new volume. I wish I had some deeply-profound, life-changing words for the occasion. Something that would provide a foolproof way to walk perfectly with God during the next six months. But….I don't.

However, I did recently read a "What does God require of us?" type of passage that can serve as a fantastic yardstick with which to measure the last six months. If you prefer, it can also work as a pretty good target to aim for in months to come.

The instructions came from the book of Micah as the prophet tried to summarize what the Lord required of His people. Micah wondered aloud if we could approach God by simply bowing down to Him, or if He required offerings of thousands of calves, rams, or rivers of oil. In reply to his own question, Micah provides the following response:

> *He has shown you, O man, what is good. And what does the Lord require of you? To act justly, to love mercy, and to walk humbly with your God.* (Micah 6:8)

Read it again…slowly this time, pausing on each requirement: Act justly…love mercy…walk humbly with God. These are "good" in the eyes of God. Which of these have you done well in the past? Which do you need to improve upon in the months to come?

Just. Merciful. Humble. May these words accurately describe each of us!

DAY 2 – THE FAITH OF JOB

We often hear about "the patience of Job" – and rightfully so. But, as I reread the account of his life, I was impressed with the <u>faith</u> of Job as well. Without the advantage of having history to look back upon as we do, Job's faith in God included an understanding of his need for an intercessor. He also understood that there was more awaiting him that far exceeded all the riches he had enjoyed on Earth.

Listen to the words of the man whom God called righteous and blameless (Job 1:1): *"Even now my Witness is in heaven; my Advocate is on high. My Intercessor is my friend as my eyes pour out tears to God; on behalf of a man He pleads with God as one pleads for a friend."* (Job 16:19-21)

Even as Job cried out in anguish over the losses he had suffered, he knew that he had a friend in heaven, an advocate who was interceding on his behalf to the Father. What a beautiful foreshadowing of the role Christ plays for us today.

Job had that hope while he languished in his horrendous circumstances. But he also had a hope beyond his current situation. *"I know that my redeemer lives, and that in the end He will stand on the earth. And after my skin has been destroyed, yet in my flesh I will see God; I myself will see Him"* (Job 19:25-27).

Friends, the same is true for us today. While we're here, we have an Advocate pleading our case before the Father. That Redeemer lives, and one day our eyes will see Him. Hope for today and hope for tomorrow; cling to it.

DAY 3 – SPRINKLED CLEAN

The class I was teaching was going through a series in the book of Exodus. When we got to the part in Chapter 24 where the Israelites affirmed their covenant with God, our pastor made an interesting point. As part of the Jews' recommitment to the covenant, young bulls were sacrificed and some of the blood sprinkled on the altar; but the rest was actually sprinkled on the people (Exodus 24:6-8).

The significance of that action can be easily missed until we consider the other times something similar was done in the Old Testament. It was done only in two very specific instances: to consecrate priests (Exodus 29), and to cleanse lepers (Leviticus 14). Blood was sprinkled on all kinds of objects on a routine basis – but only on these rare occasions was it applied to people.

No, we're not priests or lepers today, but what happened to them through the blood of a sacrifice very much applies to us. For upon being anointed by the blood, priests passed from common men to holy servants, and lepers went from being unclean to clean.

Through faith in Christ and His sacrifice on the cross, we too pass from the common to the holy. And by His blood, our sins have been washed white as snow.

Take a moment today and thank Him that you are no longer common and unclean, but holy and purified!

Cleanse me with hyssop, and I will be clean; wash me, and I will be whiter than snow. (Psalm 51:7)

DAY 4 – BROKEN IS BEAUTIFUL

The book of Leviticus is often a long, dry read. In it, God lays out the rules for His people, Israel, including instructions for temple sacrifices. There were burnt offerings, sin offerings, wave offerings, and grain offerings. Among the seemingly endless rules, however, I found something wonderful:

> It [the grain offering] must be prepared with oil on a griddle; bring it well-mixed and present the grain offering **broken in pieces** as an aroma pleasing to the Lord. (Leviticus 6:21, emphasis added)

I'm not an expert in the regulations surrounding sacrifices, but I couldn't help but smile at the wording above. Specifically, it made my heart glad to know that something broken could be pleasing to God.

You see, I know who – and what – I am. And while I may appear to have it (reasonably) put together on the outside, I'm broken and pretty flawed inside. Yet if we come to God and present all our broken pieces to Him, He will accept us. Not only are we accepted in our brokenness, but we are pleasing to Him – in our brokenness.

Yet how often do we delay going to God fearing we must "get our act together" first? I've often heard those who haven't accepted Christ say they need to "clean up their act" before God will accept them. Friends, that's a lie. Listen instead to God's truth:

> But God demonstrates his own love for us in this: While we were still sinners, Christ died for us. (Romans 5:12)

Maybe today you need to be reminded that broken is beautiful in the eyes of God. You don't need to get everything together first. Go to Him now – just the way you are.

DAY 5 – TELEPRESSURE

The article in a business journal caught my eye. Among other things, the author described a study which found that more than 50 percent of employees checked work email before and after work hours, throughout the weekend, and when sick. Even while on vacation, 44 percent checked their work email.

What's the impact? According to a Northern Illinois University study, the inability to relax and truly disengage from work produces a prolonged stress response which the researchers named "telepressure." This prolonged state of stress increases the risk of heart disease, depression, and obesity, while also decreasing cognitive performance.

Conclusion – it's harmful to us, yet we somehow cannot seem to stop! It's almost like we're addicted to our work. God understands human nature and apparently saw this day coming; therefore, He provided these instructions thousands of years ago:

> *It is a Sabbath of complete rest for you, and you must practice self-denial; it is a permanent statute.* (Leviticus 16:31, HCSB)

When we think about "self-denial" as a commandment from God, our minds may go to things like abstaining from sex or some other pleasure. But when it comes to the Sabbath, what God wants us to deny ourselves is work. Isn't that fascinating?

If you're still in the work force, may I gently ask – are you living with telepressure? If so, please remember that God's Word tells us it's okay to deny yourself (and your employer) on the weekend in order to take a break from your work. In fact, it's healthy. As you know, it will still be there on Monday morning!

DAY 6 – RECHARGING

Yesterday, we talked about the need to "unplug." The topic is so important, we need to reinforce it today!

> *Therefore we do not lose heart. Though outwardly we are wasting away, yet inwardly we are being renewed day by day.* (2 Cor 4:16)

To the best of my recollection, it's the first time both of them conked out at the same time. As I plugged both my razor and beard trimmer in, I realized that neither of them was holding a charge as long as they once did. My need to recharge them is becoming much more frequent.

While I refuse to acknowledge that I'm getting older, I must admit that my "batteries" seem to need more frequent "recharging" now too. Six hours of sleep doesn't seem to cut it like it once did. Minor scrapes and cuts take weeks to heal, and my joints just seem to ache non-stop. So, yes, I can relate to Paul's contention that *outwardly I am wasting away.*

Yet, Lord willing, the race is far from over for me. I hope to have many more laps around this track of life – more chances to share His Word and His love with others. But to be effective for Him, I need to remain connected to Him. Just like my razors need to be plugged in frequently, so too do I need to plug in to God regularly. Ideally, I'd never allow myself to become unplugged.

I have no recipe for remaining connected, but these words of Christ came to me as I was typing: "*Come with me by yourselves to a quiet place and get some rest*" (Mark 6:31).

Are your batteries running a little low? Maybe it's time to get away with Christ and let Him renew you.

DAY 7 – TREE OF LIFE

Scripture devotes a great deal of time to our words. Overall, the take-home message is that our words have the ability to bring life to others, or to destroy them (Proverbs 18:21).

Recently, while reading Proverbs 15 during my morning quiet time, I came upon this: *"A soothing tongue is a tree of life, but perversion in it crushes the spirit"* (v 4).

Again we see two possible outcomes from our words – one very positive, and the other very negative; the difference depends upon what we say and how we say it. A *soothing* tongue literally means one that brings healing to the listener. The words, and the motivation, are gentle, encouraging, and nourishing. They are wisely applied to the heart of the wounded in order to bring them back to health.

In contrast, that same tongue can bring forth different words with different motives, resulting in totally different outcomes. *Perversion* here has nothing to do with foul, filthy language, but carries the sense of *viciousness*. The words are harsh and cutting, and the motive is not to restore or heal but to further tear down. And instead of becoming a place where life is gained, these words crush the remaining spirit of the unfortunate audience.

As I was reading this passage, I happened to be sitting on my porch a few feet from the maple tree in my front yard. It was teeming with activity and life. Birds were flocking to its branches where they were finding food, rest, and shelter. Friends, when our words flow from a heart that desires to nourish others, people will want to be near us, and we can become a tree of life to them.

Your words…do they bring life to others, or do they crush them? Choose wisely.

DAY 8 – THE OUTAGE

It was only twenty-four hours – but it didn't seem like it.

The predictions of violent storms that night came as no surprise. Seeing the dark red on local radar, I gathered my family and headed to the basement. Within minutes, the tornado sirens began. As we watched the TV weatherman, the lights flickered, dimmed, and finally went out for good.

We didn't panic. We'd been in this house for twenty-six years, and collectively, power had been out for less than five hours. There was every indication that this occurrence would be no different, and we expected to be up and running in no time. After all, we could look across the street and see our neighbors had power. So we waited…and waited…and waited. Before long, we decided we'd better find the flashlights, weather radio, and the like.

We went to bed fully expecting to wake up with power. Not the case. So we improvised. We changed our routine, got out of the dark house, grabbed lunch, went to a library (which had power), and ate dinner. Finding the lights still off, we read by the light of a lantern, then played cards by the same light. We talked a bit more. We told stories and laughed. We huddled together because the house was getting cooler.

We later discovered we were one of only twenty-five homes in our town impacted. Were we unfortunate, or was it a blessing in disguise? You see, as soon as the power returned, it was "business as usual" as everyone went their separate ways. Don't get me wrong; I wouldn't want to return to days without electricity. But the temporary break from the routine was refreshing.

What would you do for twenty-four hours if you had no electricity? How might you use the time to strengthen bonds within your family or with God?

Above all, keep fervent in your love for one another… (1 Peter 4:8, NASB)

DAY 9 – A BEAUTIFUL STEP

Those who have served well gain an excellent standing….
(1Timothy 3:13)

It's one of those passages that we pull out every few years when
the need to nominate deacons comes around. While Paul was
certainly outlining the qualifications needed in those who serve as
deacons, those same qualities are things for which every Christian
should strive.

Perhaps we'll come back and look at those qualities another time,
but for today I want us to look at one of the benefits that
accompanies our Christian service (whether we hold the position
of deacon or not). Specifically, Paul tells us that those who
faithfully serve others gain *an excellent standing*.

In the original Greek, *excellent* comes from a word that means
beautiful, and *standing* from a word that described *a single step in
a staircase*. It's a place of sure footing as we climb up or down.
 In a sense, when we choose to serve others, we are taking a step
that God sees as beautiful. I can't help but think that each act of
selfless service is beautiful to God because with each such step,
we resemble Jesus a bit more. As we bend down to humbly serve
others, we take a beautiful step up toward bearing the image of
Christ.

Thankfully, nobody else needs to be aware of our service. God
sees – and our willingness to serve Him in relative anonymity is
probably even more beautiful in His eyes.

Take a moment right now and think about who in your
neighborhood, school, or church could use your help. Then take a
beautiful step and serve them.

DAY 10 – THE DIMMER SWITCH

In the same way, let your light shine before others, that they may see your good deeds and glorify your Father in heaven. (Matthew 5:16)

Like many of you, I want others to see the love and hope of Christ radiating from my life. That's the goal.

However, recently I've unintentionally reduced the brightness of my life's bulb. I just wasn't shining as I could – as I should. Unfortunate circumstances from one area of life were spilling over into several other areas. I was being mistreated, or so I believed, and I began to silently grumble.

That's when the truth below began to convict me.

> *Do everything without grumbling or arguing, so that you may become blameless and pure, "children of God without fault in a warped and crooked generation." Then you will shine among them like stars in the sky as you hold firmly to the word of life.* (Philippians 2:14-16)

Like Matthew, Paul also wrote of our ability to shine before others. Yet, our grumbling and complaining act like a dimmer switch connected directly to our bulb. Every time we grumble, argue, or complain it's like we reach over to the light switch and dim our bulb.

Please don't misunderstand: there are times for speaking up and taking necessary steps to correct a wrong, even abusive situation. But I'm referring to grumbling as a relatively constant state of affairs. Such ongoing expressions of unresolved conflict snuff out our life's light. And if we want to attract people to God, we need to shine like bright stars in a dark sky.

Give it some thought – in what ways might grumbling or arguing be harming your witness?

DAY 11 – WHOSE NAME?

It was Media Day at the 2015 Super Bowl. The biggest names in football were given the largest stage. The spotlight of success often reveals what's in the heart. One "superstar" spouted off that he was only attending the media day because he would be fined if he skipped it. Duly noted, #24.

During the game, while many eyes were on the flashy running back, I was drawn to a soft-spoken giant who also spoke on Media Day. I'd never heard of Chris Jones prior to seeing his interview. He was raised in a small town and played college ball at a relatively small school. According to his NFL team's website, "Chris Jones had an early introduction to failure in the NFL. Taken behind thirty-seven other defensive linemen in the 2013 NFL Draft, he was cut by two teams over a span of just eleven days. Rather than be deterred by these early disappointments, Jones maintained a positive outlook when he signed with the Patriots on Sept. 11, and it has paid off in a big way." That Sunday, Chris Jones was in the starting lineup at the Super Bowl. Pretty cool.

But that young man, who was literally half my age and twice my weight, hadn't lost sight of who he was or of what's important in life. Jones used his one opportunity on the largest stage of his profession to glorify his God instead of himself. Speaking about the role of football in his life, Jones said, "This is just something that I do; it's not who I am. Who I am is a Christian man who loves the Lord – and I just happen to play football." He then used the rest of his interview to encourage kids to read their Bibles!

Friends, each of us face a similar struggle each day – who or what will we live for? Will we take the credit for our worldly success and bask in the limelight? Or will we take every opportunity to bring glory to the only One who is worthy?

When given the opportunity, whose name will we proclaim?

I will proclaim the name of the Lord. Oh, praise the greatness of our God! (Deuteronomy 32:3)

DAY 12 – MY FOOD

Besides the very familiar lesson which stemmed from Jesus' interaction with the woman at the well in Samaria, there is a second lesson from that setting that we can apply to our lives today as well.

If you recall, Jesus and His disciples arrived at the well at around noon. Christ sent His men into town to buy food, and while they were gone, He encountered the woman. When the disciples returned, they encouraged Jesus to eat. His response is full of implications for us. *"I have food to eat that you do not know about…My food is to do the will of Him who sent Me and to accomplish His work"* (John 4:32,34). Jesus then went on to describe what that work was – to preach repentance among the fields leading to a harvest of eternal life (v.35).

Why would Jesus refer to doing the will of His Father as food? It certainly wasn't a reference to what is put into the belly. No, I believe Christ was referring to that which gives us energy, that which nourishes us and propels us onward toward a goal. In addition, I think He was implying that nothing else satisfies that deep hunger that burns within each of us. A hunger to know that our lives have mattered, that we lived the life He intended.

Friends, the same is true today. You were created by the Father to complete His will and accomplish His work. Knowing what God created you for, and then doing it, will nourish you and propel you forward in this life. And nothing, absolutely nothing, else will satisfy that gnawing hunger within. Only actively living for God satisfies the soul.

DAY 13 – VEXATION

Vexation – now there's a word you don't see every day! It's such a cool-sounding word – like something a TV character might use to call down curses on a foe!

But in reality, it's not a very cool thing at all. Webster defines vexation as *the state of being worried or annoyed: irritation or annoyance*. We all know that this imperfect world is full of irritations and annoyances – there truly is no escaping them. So the key with irritants is not to avoid them, but to deal with them effectively.

Thankfully, Scripture lends us some very practical advice:

> *The vexation of a fool is known at once, but the prudent ignores an insult.* (Proverbs 12:16, ESV)

In one short sentence we're given several possible responses to the irritants that come our way. Two are clearly spelled out; the other is only implied. The first option is to immediately air our irritation with others. Whether it's a private rant or an angry, "I-don't-care-what anyone-thinks" update on social media – to vent our full frustration in knee-jerk fashion is foolish.

The second defined option, which Scripture calls prudent, is to overlook the irritation altogether. Completely letting a matter go is certainly reasonable and sensible when possible. The last option is one that must be inferred from the others. This third option needs to be applied in situations that cannot be overlooked, where something must be addressed.

Notice that the proverb says that voicing our irritation "at once" is what is foolish, not that any or all communication of irritation is unwise. For those irritating situations that cannot (and should not) be ignored, taking time to relax, formulate a non-volatile response, and then communicating it calmly is sensible.

Vexation is coming – how will you handle it?

DAY 14 – WIND AND SAILS

The pessimist complains about the wind; the optimist expects it to change; the realist adjusts the sails.
-William Arthur Ward

I know little about William Ward, but I appreciate his words above. By selecting the wind for his illustration, Ward brilliantly chose something everyone is familiar with but that nobody can control. The wind therefore represents those things that inevitably come into our lives, things over which we have little or no influence. Maybe it's new management at work turning the office upside down or the doctor's report confirming your worst fear. How do we react in such conditions?

As Ward acknowledges, many of us throw up our hands and cry "No fair!" but do nothing to better our situations. We simply bemoan the intrusion of the difficulty into our world. Others are willing to endure the current setback, hoping that "better days" are just around the corner. If they can just wait it out, surely things will improve. Trust me, I understand both of these groups of people!

The last group, however, doesn't bemoan the wind or sit idly waiting for it to pass, but instead finds ways to embrace it. These people set the disappointments aside and invite God into the midst of the new reality. The realist asks Him, "Lord, how are You and I going to use this situation for my good and Your glory?" These folks are willing and able to set their dreams and disappointments aside and allow God to redirect their paths. They don't complain excessively, and they don't simply wait for things to change. Instead, they determine which way the Lord is sending the wind and they adjust their sails to travel along with Him.

Of the three groups mentioned, which best describes you? Are you willing to complain less, lay down your plans, and allow God to take your ship where He'd have it go?

Many are the plans in a person's heart, but it is the Lord's purpose that prevails. (Proverbs 19:21)

DAY 15 – CENTS OR SOULS?

I know many believers who seem to be more interested in saving a buck than they are saving a soul. They get more excited about finding a bargain than they do making a disciple!
-Steve Shadrach

Ouch – right? Believe me, I'm in the same boat. I read those words right after researching the price of an item on Ebay, Amazon, and Walmart.com. I probably spent twenty minutes trying to save twenty cents. Was it worth it? You tell me.

What might I have done with those twenty minutes that could have benefitted God's Kingdom instead? Sadly, we'll never know – because those twenty minutes are lost forever. Ironically, right now I'm looking at $1.31 in loose change just sitting on my desk – I didn't even know it was there. The twenty cents I save were so insignificant…and I repeat this routine frequently. It's almost like I expect Christ to be impressed with all the money I saved the Kingdom.

But as Shadrach contends, God is not going to ask us about our frugality. Instead, He may ask, "Why didn't you just focus on the things I commanded you to? Why did you exchange so much of your valuable and irreplaceable time on earth for something as temporal and replenishable as money?"

I'm not suggesting we throw caution to the wind; discipline in our finances is necessary and biblical. Yet if we're not careful, we may become more interested in saving a buck than saving a soul, making a dollar instead of a disciple.

Lord, help us find the right balance. Forgive us for caring more about dollars than disciples, cents more than souls.

Therefore go and make disciples of all nations, baptizing them in the name of the Father and of the Son and of the Holy Spirit (Matthew 28:19).

DAY 16 – THE CHALLENGE

The book genuinely challenged the way I view presenting the gospel to a culture that, for all intents and purposes, is running from Christians and our message. The author (accurately, I believe) took the stance that non-believers want to be loved by us, not viewed as "potential converts" only.

While that may be easy for us to agree with, it is very difficult at times to live out. Because frankly, unsaved people live like ornery, mischievous, sinful, unsaved people – in other words, just like we once did. Even without intending to, after a few years in the post-salvation camp, we end up gravitating toward those who are like-minded and like-behaved, almost to the exclusion of all others. But as Rabbi Jonathan Sacks once wrote, "The Hebrew Bible (Old Testament) in one verse commands, 'You shall love your neighbor as yourself,' but in no fewer than thirty-six places commands us to 'love the stranger.' The supreme religious challenge is to see God's image in one who is not in OUR image."

As Philip Yancey writes, "The more we love, and the more *unlikely* people we love, the more we resemble God." Want to resemble God? Love the "unlovable"…that's the challenge.

For if you love those who love you, what reward will you have? Don't even the tax collectors do the same. (Matthew 5:46)

DAY 17 – MY LIPS ARE SEALED?

Occasionally, I've heard the argument that an individual's relationship with God is a personal thing and should be kept between themselves and the Lord. While our relationship with God is certainly a personal thing, it's definitely not something we should be silent about – far from it, actually. Consider the example of King David, who in Psalm 40 wrote these words:

> *I proclaim Your saving acts in the great assembly; I do not seal my lips, Lord, as You know. I do not hide Your righteousness in my heart; I speak of Your faithfulness and Your saving help. I do not conceal Your love and Your faithfulness from the great assembly.* (vv 9-10)

It's tempting at times to remain silent, to be intimidated into concealing our belief in Christ. However, David, for one, would have no part of it. In his mind, the greatness of God – His salvation, righteousness, faithfulness, and love – demanded to be expressed. I suspect that if you were around David for any length of time, he would have told you about his awesome God. By the way, verse eight of the same chapter states that David longed to do the will of God – and apparently he saw sharing his faith with others as part of God's will for his life. It's part of His will for us as well (Mark 16:15).

So how about you? Do you seal your lips, hide His righteousness, or conceal His love and faithfulness from others? If so, what's holding you back? He's too good to keep to yourself. Look for opportunities this week!

DAY 18 – FAR OR NEAR THE TREE

I was leading a study on the life of Joseph. However, to better understand Joseph, we had to go back a bit and look at the way his parents (Jacob and Rachel) first met. Just as your story begins with your parents, the same is true for Joseph.

Although I've studied the history of Abraham, Isaac, and Jacob many times, it always amazes me how truly messed-up they were. While they were God's chosen people, theirs was not the type of family we'd choose! There were generations of deceit, jealousy, manipulation, and parental favoritism. In many cases, the apple just didn't fall too far from the tree.

But when we get to Joseph, we see the end of many of the family's harmful cycles. Although his family was undoubtedly not perfect, we don't see multiple spouses, bickering siblings, or favoritism played among children. While we may never know for sure, perhaps God sent Joseph away from his family of origin, in part, so he could have a fresh beginning. Regardless, we can clearly see the results – Joseph's children did not carry the same baggage as prior generations.

As I considered this truth, I was encouraged that the same opportunity exists today. None of us come from perfect families, but none of us are doomed to repeat the mistakes of our parents, either. <u>For while the apple may not fall too far from the tree, it DOESN'T have to grow there!</u> With God's help, we have the ability to chart a new course in a single generation!

Give it some thought – what traits from your family are worth carrying forward? Water those seeds. What traits should not be a part of future generations? Pull those out by the roots.

Now behold, he has a son who has observed all his father's sins which he committed, and observing does not do likewise. (Ezekiel 18:14, NASB)

DAY 19 – HARD HEARTS AND TIGHT FISTS

If anyone is poor among your fellow Israelites in any of the towns of the land the LORD *your God is giving you, do not be hardhearted or tightfisted toward them.* (Deuteronomy 15:7)

Hardhearted and tightfisted. If taken by themselves, they are words we'd never want to be used of us. Yet that is so often our reaction to the poor we encounter around us. A *hard heart* is one that has become calloused against the poor and needy. A hardened heart looks for the faults in others that led to their condition and judges what they find. And as our hearts close toward others, our hands and wallets close as well.

By this time, you've likely heard me say it before – when Scripture tells us NOT to do one thing, it generally provides a better alternative shortly thereafter. Such is also the case here. If we're not to close our hearts and our hands to those in need, what is the response God desires? Here it is:

> *Rather, be openhanded and freely lend them whatever they need.* (v.8)

Openhanded and freely lending. Wouldn't you rather be known by such terms? Both can be boiled down to one quality – generosity. An *open hand* is just what it sounds like – *placing what one has in the palm of their hand for others to take or borrow.* This is done *freely* – without judgment or strings attached.

Please understand that this was done in the context of community (Israelite to Israelite within the same town); this is not a command to let any stranger take our "stuff." But the right condition of the heart is what God is after. Do you perceive and hold your possessions with a hard heart and tight fist? Or are you openhanded and willing to lend?

David's life was unraveling. One son, Amnon, had raped David's daughter, Tamar. David knew about it but did nothing. As a result, a second son, Absalom, avenged his sister by killing Amnon. All of these events occurred after David committed adultery with Bathsheba and murdered Uriah. So much for the man after God's own heart!

But the family's troubles were far from over. Next, Absalom led a revolt, setting himself up as king in David's place. As David fled Jerusalem, his priests encouraged him to take the Ark of the Covenant with him.

It was a moment of major decision, the sort that arrives only a few times in life – yet alters the rest of the journey. In that moment, David could have taken the Ark, mustered his army, and fought against his son. Many say he should have. Yet David took a different path – one that on the surface looked like defeat but actually demonstrated tremendous strength and victory.

To the priests offering the Ark, David replied:

> *If I find favor in the Lord's eyes, He will bring me back and allow me to see both it and its dwelling place. However, if He should say, "I do not delight in you," then here I am— He can do with me whatever pleases Him. (2 Samuel 15:25-26)*

In that moment, David hadn't surrendered to Absalom; he had surrendered to God. David knew that God was disciplining him and it might end in defeat – or it might lead to victory – but the outcome was going to be the Lord's decision, not David's. Therefore, David placed himself in God's hands and said, "Here I am – do with me whatever pleases You."

Because "surrender" often feels like defeat, we generally resist it with every fiber of our being. But is there any safer, better place to be than within God's hands? Remember, we place ourselves there through our daily voluntary surrender to Him.

DAY 21 – 185 DAYS

Today, my oldest brother begins his thirty-first (and last) year of teaching high school biology. For more than three decades he has devoted himself to the education of the students in his hometown. One career, spent in one school district, and today he begins his last lap around that track.

When I talked to him about it recently, he smiled and just said, "185 days" (apparently he's going to count them down this year). When specifically asked what was going to be next for him, he shrugged somewhat and simply said, "I really don't know. But there will be something!"

Please don't get me wrong. My brother loves teaching, and he cares deeply about his students and their success. But as much as he has enjoyed all those years and all those students, he's ready for whatever comes next. As I listened to him, I couldn't help but think of how similar it is to my own longing for what's next.

As much as I love and enjoy a great deal of my life here, there is still a pent-up excitement for what lies ahead. I won't wish away my remaining days here, and I may not even be able to picture what God has in store, but I can smile when I think of the days ahead because I know the best is truly yet to come. All of which reminds me of a song that I've always found encouraging, Scott Krippayne's "The Best is Yet to Come." Look it up on YouTube if you have a few minutes; you will be blessed.

For God's children, the best is definitely yet to come!

What no eye has seen, what no ear has heard, and what no human mind has conceived the things God has prepared for those who love him. (1 Corinthians 2:9)

"I've got music/I've got rhythm/I've got my gal/who could ask for anything more?" Well, frankly, I think I could! George and Ira Gershwin wrote a very memorable song, but music, rhythm, and even a gal aren't things that satisfy for long. No, we need something much more permanent and stable to make it through this life.

Recently, I came across something that answers the deeper longings of this thirsty soul:

> *The Lord is close to the brokenhearted and saves those who are crushed in spirit.* (Psalm 34:18)

Pause for just a moment and read those promises again. First, we see that God is close – the original language conveys the idea of *one's closest neighbor* or *friend who comes* near, perhaps when the rest of the world is walking out. Next, we see that He *saves* us. In the broadest of terms, it means that He *delivers us from tight, confining spots*, and places us in wide-open areas of freedom.

Notice, however, that these promises are for those who are brokenhearted (*shattered, broken*) and crushed in spirit (*humble, contrite*). To those who have been shattered, broken, and humbled by life, God says He will draw near and set us free.

As I read Psalm 34, I found myself humming it to the tune above. "I've got my Lord, He saves my soul. He stays near me, who could ask for anything more?!"

To the broken and crushed, remember He is near.

DAY 23 – HIS PORTION

It's a perspective we perhaps don't allow ourselves to consider very often. Yet it's one that God reminds us of frequently.

As Moses transferred the mantle of leadership to Joshua, he passed along these words: "*Be strong and courageous, for you must go with this people into the land that the Lord swore to their ancestors to give them, and you must divide it among them as their inheritance*" (Deuteronomy 31:7).

Shortly after those words about the people's inheritance, Moses went on to say something very revealing. Pay special attention to these next words:

> *The Lord's portion is His people, Jacob His allotted inheritance.* (32:9)

When God made His covenant with Abraham, He promised the people their land and His blessing. All God wanted and received in return was THEM! God considered the people of His covenant to be His portion and His inheritance. He wanted nothing more.

The same is true today. God's desire is for all men to enter into the new covenant He offers in Christ. Those who do gain everything, and He gains us – yet somehow, He considers that a "good deal" from His perspective.

Give it some thought today – if God were asked what He would like to inherit as His very own, His answer would be YOU! You are His delight.

DAY 24 – CORNERS

In *The Problem of Pain,* C.S. Lewis writes, "They [Adam and Eve] wanted some corner in the universe of which they could say to God, 'This is our business, not Yours.' But there is no such corner."

I suspect that Lewis is correct – from the dawn of time, men have wanted to separate life into the sacred and the secular. There are days and times in which God is "allowed:" Sunday mornings, prayer time around the dinner table, the waiting room of any hospital. However, the rest of our time is seen as just that – ours, to be lived as we see fit, free from the interference of God. If we're honest, it's God who has a little corner, and we expect Him to stay in it!

Believe me, I get it; I love to retain ownership whenever I can. It has taken me years to realize that while my life INVOLVES me, it's not ABOUT me. The same is true for you.

In the end it's a matter of lordship – who gets to control what in our lives. Will it be us, or will it be God? As someone once said, "Jesus is either Lord of all, or He is not at all." But unfortunately, the old man doesn't die easily. It's not a "one and done" proposition. At every decision point each day, we are faced with the question of whose plans will prevail – ours or God's.

In this moment, be honest with yourself – have you attempted to place God in a corner? Is He Lord of ALL your life? If not, what part or parts are you holding back from Him?

...no one can say, "Jesus is Lord," except by the Holy Spirit. (1 Corinthians 12:3)

DAY 25 – THE UN-LAZY RIVER

After we exited our community center's pool, another swimmer suggested that if I wanted a REAL workout, I should spend some time in the adjacent "lazy river." But instead of floating along with the current, I was to walk against it.

To be honest, I thought *How hard can THAT be*? Well, I was wrong! There was absolutely NOTHING lazy about going against the lazy river's current! From the moment I stepped into the river's flow, its current tried to push me downstream. It truly was all I could do to stand in one place. In fact, simply standing there became impossible. I was either going to be swept along with the current, or I was going to have to turn into the man-made rapids and surge upstream.

For the next 30 minutes I forced myself against the tide. I was the only person going that direction and the others who floated lazily past me gave me that "What-are-you-doing-weirdo?" look! When I finished, my body felt battered and my feet were literally torn up – they worked extra hard trying to push against the pool's floor.

My point today has nothing to do with a physical workout, yet the "lazy river" provides a wonderful analogy to the Christian walk. When we accept Jesus as our Lord, He invites us to walk with Him. Friends, that walk is almost always upstream, against the world's current. Our culture wants to drag us downstream, away from God and His Son. And there really isn't an option to just "stay put." We will either float along with the world, or we'll turn against that current and walk upstream!

Take a few minutes and ask yourself what you're doing with the culture's current…are you allowing it to float you further and further from Christ? Or are you walking upstream? Any changes you need to make?

You adulterous people, don't you know that friendship with the world means enmity against God? Therefore, anyone who chooses to be a friend of the world becomes an enemy of God. (James 4:4)

DAY 26 – A PRETTY PROBLEM

From the earliest of days, men have struggled with what I'll call the "pretty problem." We desperately want to be considered among the pretty people, and if we can't, we at least want to be associated with them.

We give such preference to those who are attractive, that there is a well-known and well-accepted, phenomenon called the "halo effect." For example, a tall or good-looking person is perceived as being more intelligent and trustworthy, even though there is no logical reason to believe height or appearance correlates with intelligence or honesty. In other words, if we're satisfied with the outside, we'll see whatever we want to see on the inside – at least initially.

That was precisely the problem Samuel faced when he went to anoint King Saul's successor. When Jesse's oldest son, Eliab, passed before him, Samuel just knew this had to be the next king. Why? He was tall and good-looking! But God's response to Samuel should serve as both a guideline and a warning to us today:

> *Do not look at his appearance or at the height of his stature, because I have rejected him; for God sees not as man sees, for man looks at the outward appearance, but the Lord looks at the heart.* (1 Samuel 16:7).

While Samuel liked what he saw on the outside, God was looking within to the heart, and what He saw there made Him reject the man. Something within Eliab's heart caused God to literally abhor what He saw.

Friends, when evaluating others to fill major roles in your life – spouse, business partner, close friend, etc. – heed God's warning. Look past the appearance into the heart. Choose character over cuteness. In the end, that's what will determine the type of relationship you'll have.

DAY 27 – OVERFLOWING JOY

I wonder, if like me, you've ever thought or said something like this: "Someday, I'll be able to give my time and/or money to ______________. Someday…"

Someday, I'll give a little money to that charity. *Someday*, I'll volunteer for that ministry that is always looking for additional helpers. *Someday*, I'll be in a better place where I'll have more time and more money.

Sound familiar? If so, you're not alone. I get it – really, I do. Perhaps that's why I found Paul's description of what the churches in Macedonia did for the struggling church in Jerusalem so incredible. Everything about what they did was so foreign to my way of thinking.

First, they gave without being asked (2 Corinthians 8:4). In fact, the new Christians in places like Philippi practically begged for the opportunity to help their fellow believers. Next, they didn't wait for a great time to involve themselves or for there to be a surplus before they chose to participate. Scripture tells us that they gave *"in the midst of a very severe trial…"* and *"their extreme poverty welled up in rich generosity"* (v2).

Let's be honest – times of severe trial and extreme poverty don't generally prompt generosity. If only our humanity were at work, we'd have to conclude such giving would be impossible. But there were two other elements at work in these believers' kindness: God's grace enabled them to do so, and they overflowed with joy related to the grace God had shown them (through the forgiveness of their sins, and provision of their needs).

Friends, does your joy over what God has done for you overflow in practical ways that help others?

PS – I'm not asking for money!

DAY 28 – LOUDER

It's a fascinating account. Jesus and His disciples were leaving Jericho on their way to Jerusalem when they encountered two blind men sitting by the road. Matthew tells us that a great crowd was following Christ, and while the blind men couldn't see Him, they obviously heard the commotion. After figuring out that the uproar was due to Jesus, the blind men cried out, *"Lord, Son of David, have mercy on us!"* (Matthew 20:30).

Amazingly, instead of taking the ones in need to the only One who could meet their need, the crowd "rebuked them and told them to be quiet" (v.31). Stop and think about that for a moment. We live in a day and age when the masses are telling those seeking Christ to be quiet. When they do, how are we to respond?

I suppose there may be different answers based on the circumstances, but I was encouraged by the response of those two blind men. Instead of giving in to the pressure of the majority, Scripture says, *"…they shouted all the louder, "'Lord, Son of David, have mercy on us!'"* (v. 31).

Unlike the crowd that wanted to silence and dismiss the blind men, Jesus stopped and healed them. Their faith and persistence brought them to Christ, and Christ's compassion and power brought sight to them!

Friends, don't let the crowds discourage you from seeking the Lord we all so desperately need. Pursue Him all the more. Through faithful persistence, great things can happen!

DAY 29 – NET WORTH

Your worth consists in what you are, not in what you have.
-Thomas Edison

Boy, do I need that reminder frequently. Ever since I was a small child, I measured my sense of well-being and worth based on what I had. I had my prized bicycle and my prized toy train set. I had good grades and good attendance at school, and so on.

As I became older, the measuring sticks of my worth changed. Soon the things I possessed became my college diploma, my job, my paycheck, my bank account, my cars, my house, and similar such things. In part, I suppose we do this because it's a cultural norm. But I wonder how much of our gathering "stuff" occurs because it's much easier to measure what we have than who, or what, we are.

It's hard to measure the goodness of our heart. It's difficult to quantify our attitudes and motives. Where's the chart for graphing our character development, our love, or our caring for others? It's much easier to log in to an online banking account and check the balance there – so we may tend to give more time and attention to such things. But just because it's easier doesn't make it better.

While Edison was acutely wise, an even wiser Man put it this way:

> *Watch out! Be on your guard against all kinds of greed; life does not consist in an abundance of possessions.* (Luke 12:15)

Be honest with yourself – how are you measuring your life and your worth? Is it by who you are or what you have?

Hezekiah inherited a MESS! Ahaz, the king of Judah before him, had ruled for sixteen years. During that time, Ahaz had erected idols to Baal and Asherah, and even sacrificed his own sons to these gods (2 Chronicles 28). That was the situation which King Hezekiah walked into.

While the condition of Judah at the beginning of his reign was not Hezekiah's FAULT, he realized it was his RESPONSIBILITY. So he wasted no time in beginning the clean-up. Listen to the way Scripture records his sense of urgency in correcting what was wrong:

> *They began the consecration on the first day of the first month, and by the eighth day of the month they reached the portico of the Lord. For eight more days they consecrated the temple of the Lord itself, finishing on the sixteenth day of the first month.* (2 Chronicles 29:17)

On the very first day of his reign, Hezekiah began consecrating the Lord's temple, which Ahaz had defiled. Day One – you simply can't start any sooner than that!

Friends, here's my point today – Scripture says that you and I are the temple of God (1 Corinthians 3:16) – and if our part of the temple needs cleaning, we shouldn't wait. We must not put off until tomorrow what God desires to see consecrated to Him today. And while some of the mess in your world may not be your fault, might it be your responsibility to fix?

Today is Day One – any part of your temple that needs your attention?

DAY 31 – WHAT TO GIVE

Ever wonder what God wants from you? Ever ask, "What is God's will for me?" While there are obviously many possible answers to these questions, we shouldn't overlook the answers that are clearly spelled out for us.

One such example is in Psalm 50. In that passage, God is telling the writer that while He has no problem with man's sacrifices, He really has no need for them. Listen as God puts it into perspective for us:

> *I have no need of a bull from your stall or of goats from your pens, for every animal of the forest is mine, and the cattle on a thousand hills. I know every bird in the mountains, and the insects in the fields are mine. If I were hungry I would not tell you, for the world is mine, and all that is in it. (50:9-12)*

Talk about not knowing what to give the Guy who has everything! So what is it that mere men can take to God that pleases Him? Great question; glad you asked! More importantly, God is happy to answer.

> *Sacrifice thank offerings to God, fulfill your vows to the Most High, and call on me in the day of trouble; I will deliver you, and you will honor me. (50:14-15).*

What does God desire from His children? That we express our thanks to Him and that we call on Him (not others or ourselves) during our trouble. When we thank Him, we honor Him (50:23), and when we call on Him, He delights to deliver us.

I can attest that little brings an earthly father more pleasure than to come to the aid of his children and to be thanked for his care and provision. Want to honor God today? Call on Him and thank Him.

DAY 32 – THE EXAMPLE

It was the night before His death, and as Jesus shared the Passover meal with His disciples, He did the unthinkable. Somewhere between the appetizers and dessert, Jesus got up from the table and began to wash the dirty, stinkin' feet of those twelve men. When He finished, Christ told His followers, *"Now that I, your Lord and Teacher, have washed your feet, you also should wash one another's feet. I have set you an example that you should do as I have done for you"* (John 13:14-15).

Over the years, I've seen some sincere, yet pretty awkward attempts to obey Jesus' instructions. In fact, I've conducted an old-fashioned foot-washing in my own classroom. However, the more I consider it, the more I'm convinced that clean feet weren't really the point of Jesus' actions or His words. Perhaps washing feet isn't the example we're actually to follow.

When we look at the context, we see that Jesus pointed out that He, the teacher, was serving them, the students. Therefore, they – the leaders of the future church – were to humble themselves in whatever way necessary in order to serve others. Humble service – THAT was the example they were to follow. And that's the example we are to follow as well.

Yes, sometimes that may mean stooping down and literally getting our hands dirty. Undoubtedly, it will mean checking our pride at the door and placing the needs of others ahead of our own. But if the Son of God was willing to do it, shouldn't we, His children, be all the more willing?

By the way, Jesus ended His instructions to His disciples with this promise: *"Now that you know these things, you will be blessed if you do them"* (v.16). I believe the same is true today.

DAY 33 – IT'S JUST FUEL

When I was young, I incorrectly learned that "money is the root of all evil." Not until I was considerably older did I realize that what Paul had actually said to his protégé, Timothy, was this:

> *...the love of money is a root of all kinds of evils.* (1 Timothy 6:10, ESV)

There is definitely a connection between money and evil, but money itself is not the issue. It's really *the love of* it that paves the way into all kinds of trouble. Not long ago, I came across a related Proverb that I'd somehow missed previously. Listen to the words of Solomon:

> *The wage of the righteous leads to life, the gain of the wicked to sin.* (Proverbs 10:16)

Here again we see that money (*wages* or *gain*) is neutral. It is only fuel that is burned up within the heart of the one who possesses it. It feeds the desires of the heart and produces the natural outcomes of what resides within. Those who are in right standing with God will use their possessions in ways that bring life to themselves and to others. Alternatively, the ungodly will use what they have in sinful ways that bring trouble – again to themselves and others.

Take a moment today and consider what the resources in your life are producing – life, or trouble and discontentment. Remember, money is neutral, but it does reveal what's within our hearts.

He was about to be silent for approximately 400 years (the time between the Old and New Testament periods). But before He did so, God wanted to address a concern He saw among His children. The Lord had this to say about the high rate of divorce among the Israelites:

> *Has not the one God made you? You belong to him in body and spirit. And what does the one God seek? Godly offspring. So be on your guard, and do not be unfaithful to the wife of your youth.* (Malachi 2:15)

I was particularly drawn to the command to "be on your guard" in the verse above. Malachi repeats the same command in verse 16, so it must be very important and key to remaining faithful. But, what exactly does it mean?

Other translations give us a slightly better understanding. The ESV, for example, says to, "guard yourselves in your spirit," while the NET Bible says, "Be attentive, then, to your own spirit." Obviously what needs to be guarded is our spirits.

The Hebrew word here, *ruach*, means *wind, spirit*, or *breath*. What these have in common is that they're unseen and often difficult to corral. In fact, as used in the verse above, the word *spirit* means, *unaccountable and uncontrollable impulse*. In other words, when it comes to protecting your marriage, watch out for those things which you don't want to be held accountable for and those impulses that you find difficult to control.

While there are certainly other issues that get couples into trouble – finances and difficulty resolving conflict, for example – it is often the "little things" we don't keep above the table that pose the greatest risk.

Take a moment and identify the unseen, uncontrollable winds that threaten your marriage…now guard yourself against them.

DAY 35 – GEORGE WILSON

George Wilson. Although you probably don't recognize his name, countless people repeat his unbelievable decision every day.

According to *Smithsonian Magazine*, in April 1830 Wilson was found guilty of robbery, obstructing delivery of the mail, and endangering the lives of mail carriers. Wilson and his partner, James Porter, were sentenced to death. Porter was hanged that July, but thanks to the lobbying of friends, Wilson received a full pardon from President Andrew Jackson. But for reasons unknown, Wilson refused the pardon.

The case went to the Supreme Court to determine if a citizen even had the right to reject a presidential pardon. The U.S. Attorney General who argued the case stated, "It is hardly necessary to speculate on the case of a man refusing to accept a pardon in a capital case. It is an event not even possible, where the party was in his sound mind." In other words, one would have to be crazy to refuse a pardon in a capital case. Yet the court ruled it had no power to impose a pardon, concluding, "A pardon…is not complete without acceptance." In the end, Wilson was hanged.

Even now I can't fathom the decision. Why would anyone choose to die when a second chance was available? Wilson was guilty, but the one person who could set him free was extending a full pardon to him. All he needed to do was accept it. But he refused.

I can think of no better illustration of the pardon offered by God through Christ. Like George Wilson, every person is guilty, yet every person has been offered an undeserved pardon through Christ. But we need to accept that free gift. Don't be a George Wilson; be pardoned instead!

> *For if, by the trespass of the one man, death reigned through that one man, how much more will those who receive God's abundant provision of grace and of the gift of righteousness reign in life through the one man, Jesus Christ!* (Romans 5:17)

DAY 36 – ON THE ROOF

There aren't too many things I dislike more than being alone for long. Yes, I need some quiet time, but after too much of it, I kind of shrivel up. So it would take quite a bit for me to seek prolonged isolation. Perhaps that's not true of others, but it is of me.

However, Scripture gives an actual reason to seek banishment to the corner of a roof or the unpleasantness of a desert. Just what could be so awful to make living alone in a desert look like a treat?

According to Proverbs 19, it's living with a quarrelsome person. Yes, technically, it points out that it is the quarrelsome wife who is to be avoided, but there's no reason to believe that life with a quarrelsome husband would be any more pleasant. But what makes a person *quarrelsome?* It must be more than the occasional disagreements that affect every relationship from time to time. Not wanting to be a quarrelsome person, I decided to look up what it meant.

The word describes a person *characterized by strife, arguing, and contention.* Interestingly, the origin of the word gives us better insight to the meaning of this proverb. *Quarrelsome* comes from a word that means *to judge,* and in this proverb it describes someone who *plays the judge in every situation.* They have an opinion on every topic – but not just any opinion; they have THE opinion – and they will defend that opinion at most any cost. Unfortunately, they seem unable to distinguish between their opinion and the gospel truth. Sadly, while defending their turf, they drive others away – far away.

Remember, check your opinions at the door and allow God to be Judge. Then let's just try to get along!

> *It is better to live in a desert land than with a quarrelsome and fretful woman.* (Proverb 21:19)

DAY 37 – JUST A LITTLE BIT MORE

I can no longer find the survey, but years ago a poll was taken asking people to estimate how much money they would need to be happy and satisfied. The results were not exactly surprising, yet are still very insightful. Regardless of the respondents' baseline income, their "target" annual revenue was always double what they had. In other words, those who were making 25,000 dollars wanted 50,000; those making 50,000 wanted 100,000; those making 100,000 wanted $200,000 and so forth.

Is there any cap to this craving? Apparently not. John D. Rockefeller, who was the wealthiest person alive in his day, was once asked, "How much money is enough?" He reportedly answered, "Just a little bit more." Solomon, who was also the richest man of day warned us of this:

"*Whoever loves money never has money enough; whoever loves wealth is never satisfied with his income*" (Ecclesiastes 5:10). And Paul told Timothy, "*For the love of money is a root of all kinds of evil. Some people, eager for money, have wandered from the faith and pierced themselves with many griefs*" (1 Timothy 6:10). Christ weighed in on the topic telling us that we cannot love both God and money; we will hate the one and serve the other (Luke 16:13).

Notice that none of these passages say that money is bad – the Lord knows we need it to survive. It is the love of money, the incessant desire for more, and the willingness to pursue money instead of God that are the trouble. The answer I believe is thankfulness and contentment – both lead to a deep satisfaction in God that money cannot buy.

Take a moment and consider your attitude toward money. Are you content and thankful for what you have? Or are you always craving more?

DAY 38 – BURNING THE CANDLE

He was a hero – yet likely nobody knew he'd done a thing.

Jethro was the father-in-law of Moses, and just a few months into their Exodus out of Egypt, he paid a visit to the Hebrew's camp. What he saw concerned him:

> *The next day Moses took his seat to serve as judge for the people, and they stood around him from morning till evening.* (Exodus 18:13)

You need to understand, there were over 600,000 men in the camp (plus women and children), but only one judge – Moses. So everyone who had a case to be settled took a number and waited for Moses to become available. It was very inefficient – plus, both Moses and the people were getting cranky.

Moses was a big man on campus – in fact he was THE big man on that campus, and it would take another very big man to challenge his practices. But that's exactly what Jethro did:

> *Moses' father-in-law replied, "What you are doing is not good. You and these people who come to you will only wear yourselves out. The work is too heavy for you; you cannot handle it alone."* (vv. 17-18)

To Moses' credit, he didn't become defensive; he became responsive. Scripture states that "*Moses listened and did everything Jethro said*" (v. 24).

Folks, sometimes we need to play the role of Jethro and step in when we see others traveling down a path that is not going to end well. Other times we may find ourselves in the role of Moses, needing to hear that the work is too much for us and that we can't handle it alone.

Any "Moses"es you need to warn today? Perhaps you're the one trying to burn the candle at both ends – remember, the one who does generally gets burned!

DAY 39 – THE WINDSHIELD

The meme told a great truth: "There's a reason the rearview mirror is so small and the windshield is so large."

We can't effectively go forward if we're constantly staring in the rearview mirror. Folks, we all have things in our pasts we wish were not there. Every single one of us. But once we have repented of them, there remains no reason to look upon them any longer. You need not focus on my past mistakes; I need not focus on yours. Perhaps more importantly, however, is our need to stop reliving our own "stuff."

If Christ's forgiveness is to have a practical impact on our todays and our tomorrows, we must stop looking back on our yesterdays. He longs for us to take what He's done for us and apply it to our lives NOW. Forgiveness of our sins isn't something that benefits us only in eternity. It frees us today! Christ wants us, from this day forward, to look in His direction. We're to fix our eyes on Him – the founder and perfecter of our faith (Hebrews 12:2). To do so we must look straight ahead…through the windshield.

If you must, cast but an occasional glance in the rearview mirror as a reminder of Christ's goodness to you, then put the car in "Drive" and move forward.

> *…let us also lay aside every weight, and sin which clings so closely, and let us run with endurance the race that is set before us, looking to Jesus, the founder and perfecter of our faith…(Hebrews 12:1-2, ESV)*

It had started nearly fifty years earlier in Stalag 3-B in Furstenberg, Germany. As the only dentist among nearly 25,000 POWs, Dr. Nikita Aseyev befriended scores of American soldiers as he performed dental procedures on them.

During their dental visits, Dr. Aseyev told his American patients of the hardships his fellow Russian POWs experienced on their side of the fence. Namely, Russians were dying of starvation at an alarming rate. Because rations were on a "per prisoner" basis, the Russians often stood corpses up during roll call in order to receive the dead's portion of food. The Americans didn't have much themselves, but the Red Cross delivered extra rations to them on a weekly basis. Instead of keeping it all, they decided to share.

According to Dr. Aseyev, several young Americans, led by Michael and Peter Wowczuk and William Jarema, began an "underground food operation." And for the better part of three years, the Americans and their dentist accomplice smuggled food to the Russians. Each realized that getting caught would bring death to all involved. At one point the Gestapo caught wind of the operation, but according to Dr. Aseyev, not one of the 8,000 American soldiers would reveal the names of the prisoners involved.

Recalling the underground project decades later, Jarema stated, "It was a terrific operation. Terrific. We were repaid many times by our feeling of satisfaction, knowing we helped people in need… If you've ever been starving yourself, you can't just walk away from a person who's starving. We were all in trouble in that camp, and we did everything we could to help one another. There ought to be more of that in the world today."

Lord, use us to bring more of that in the world today!

> *Do nothing out of selfish ambition or vain conceit. Rather, in humility value others above yourselves, not looking to your own interests but each of you to the interests of the others.* (Philippians 2:3-4)

DAY 41 – DOUBLE VICTORY

In a sermon entitled: "Loving Your Enemies," Martin Luther King, Jr. wrote the following:

"To our most bitter opponents we say, "'…Do to us what you will, and we shall continue to love you... Throw us in jail and we shall still love you. Bomb our homes and threaten our children, and we shall still love you. Send your hooded perpetrators of violence into our community at the midnight hour and beat us and leave us half dead, and we shall still love you…One day we shall win freedom, but not only for ourselves. We shall so appeal to your heart and conscience that we shall win you in the process and our victory will be a double victory.'"

What a beautiful message on the power of love. Perhaps even more amazing than the words, however, is the fact that King wrote them from a prison cell during the Montgomery bus conflict. And so important was it to King that this message be shared that, against doctor's orders, he took the pulpit one Sunday morning in November 1957 when he delivered this sermon at Dexter Avenue Baptist Church. He was so sick that he arrived only in time to deliver the message and then was immediately ordered back to bed.

As I read King's words, I wondered what my approach was to "winning over" my enemies. Do I try to beat them into submission through well-worded arguments? Do I drive them away with hateful words and actions? Do I ignore them, silently hoping they will go away? Or do I, like King, appeal to their hearts and attempt to win a double victory by relentlessly loving them?

Christ's approach was love – what's yours?

> *You have heard that it was said, "Love your neighbor and hate your enemy." But I tell you, love your enemies and pray for those who persecute you, that you may be children of your Father in heaven. (Matt 5:43-45)*

While much is made over Absalom's rebellion against his father King David, we hear far less about a second rebellion led immediately thereafter by Sheba, a grandson of King Saul.

After gathering men to join in his attempted coup, Sheba ended up within the walls of a city in northern Israel known for the wisdom of its inhabitants. While Sheba and his men huddled inside, David's men were huffing and puffing to break the door down! If something wasn't done quickly to bring peace, many lives would be lost in the ensuing battle.

At that time, an anonymous woman of the city stepped forward and said, *"I am one of those who are peaceable and faithful in Israel"* (2 Samuel 20:19). She then brokered a deal that ushered in peace and cost but one life (that of Sheba).

As I studied this scene, I was intrigued by the concept of being *peaceable.* The original language conveys the meaning of *entering into covenants of peace; the quality of being a peace maker.* Someone who is peaceable not only strives for peace within their own life, but they also help others see that they are able to enter into peace as well – and there's a big difference.

If I'm **only** interested in living peacefully myself, I intentionally **won't** interject myself into the lives of other people. Why? Because involving myself with others can get messy and erode my peaceful life. But if I'm a maker of peace, if I broker peace between people at odds, then I will temporarily set my personal peace aside to help others achieve peace of their own.

PeaceABLE – what a wonderful quality to possess. No wonder Jesus said the peacemakers would be called sons of God (Matthew 5:9).

I can't believe it. I just can't believe it. When it happened last year, I vowed it would NEVER HAPPEN AGAIN. Guess what? It just happened – AGAIN!

For whatever reason, my county chooses to send notices for personal property and real estate taxes in late November or early December. It's a busy time of year for all of us, and well…the bills got overlooked and were paid late.

I'm embarrassed to admit it, but last year my delinquency cost me several hundred dollars. And if there's anything I hate more than paying taxes, it's giving the government extra money in late fees! It was so irritating last year that I was going to do whatever it took to prevent a repeat performance. But, alas, I did it again. This time, however, I noticed it much earlier – so my fine was ONLY half that from last year. But still…UGH!

My painful, expensive oversights came to mind when I read the following: "…*the complacency of fools destroys them*" (Proverbs 1:32). No, I wasn't completely destroyed but, boy, was my complacency foolish and destructive.

Complacency in this verse conveys a sense of security arising from abundance, peace, or prosperity. It's that sense of living so abundantly that you don't need to pay close attention to the details. It's being fooled into a false sense of security that results in carelessness in our actions. I wonder, too, if it might involve a presumption on our part of God's continued blessings. I guarantee you if I needed that money to put groceries on my table, I wouldn't have missed those bills!

How about you? Have you allowed your relative abundance to make you complacent in any area? Heed Scripture's warning – be careful; complacency will destroy us if it goes unchecked.

DAY 44 – CENTER STAGE

We don't talk about it much, but suffering is a part of life. And our capacity to endure it sometimes depends on our willingness to view it within a bigger picture.

We're familiar with the story of the Israelites' Exodus. We know Pharaoh refused several orders to release the Hebrews, leading to the infamous ten plagues. And as a result of those plagues, people suffered. The Israelites continued to suffer as slaves, and the Egyptians suffered the loss of life, limb, and property.

Before the plagues even started, God revealed His purpose, which includes a key to understanding suffering.

> *And the Egyptians will know that I am the Lord when I stretch out my hand against Egypt and bring the Israelites out of it.* (Exodus 7:5)

The longer Pharaoh delayed, the longer the people suffered. But notice the outcome of the suffering – the Egyptians would know that God is Lord! Sometimes (and only sometimes), God allows suffering so that He can become known through it. Hebrews 5:8 says that Jesus learned obedience through what He suffered, and certainly God became better known through Christ.

About the man born blind, Jesus said, *"It was not that this man sinned, or his parents, but that the works of God might be displayed in him"* (John 9:3). In 1 Peter 1:6-7, the apostle wrote, *"In this you rejoice, though now for a little while, if necessary, you have been grieved by various trials, so that the tested genuineness of your faith—more precious than gold that perishes though it is tested by fire—may be found to result in praise and glory and honor at the revelation of Jesus Christ."*

You see, our suffering is an arena where God can take center stage. Our trials are opportunities for Christ to become better known. What if we could begin to see our trials not as setbacks to ourselves but as ways to advance our Lord's name?

DAY 45 – DO THEY CARE?

Several years ago, Christian researcher George Barna published the results of a national survey focused on those unaffiliated with any church (aka "the unchurched"). Among the many other fascinating revelations were the responses to the question, "What would seek in a church if you were to look for one?"

The number-one answer, ahead of the theological beliefs of the church, the quality of programs for children, church involvement in helping poor, coffee bar at the welcome area, or even the quality of the sermons and music, was this:

<u>Do the people seem to care for one another</u>?

Certainly the qualities mentioned above are important for a church. However, what the unchurched want to see is whether "this whole Christian thing" really makes a difference in the lives of those who claim to have it. Specifically, does what we claim to believe translate into genuine love for people?

Coffee, comfortable seats, quality music, and good sermons won't keep people at a church if they don't readily experience real care and love. An unloved church member will soon become an uninvolved church member, and eventually they'll leave in search of a more loving environment.

It's no wonder Jesus kept it short and to the point when He said, *"This is my command: Love each other"* (John 15:17). It's just that simple and just that hard!

May I ask a difficult question today? If your church was only as loving as you are personally, how loving would an "outsider" conclude your church is?

DAY 46 – CHANGES

Change stinks! If it were left up to me, we'd still be riding horses and cooking over open fires! Obviously, many changes have wonderfully improved our lives. But those aren't the types of changes I'm referencing. The ones I dislike are the big ones that drastically alter my comfort.

Things like a child leaving home, or losing a job because the company office moved to Jersey. Perhaps the change we hated to see was a loved one dying or a friend moving away. Changes that we didn't choose, but in many ways were forced upon us.

Author Mary Shelley wrote, "Nothing is so painful to the human mind as a great and sudden change." In many ways I agree. Large and abrupt changes make us stop and ask God what He's up to. Such changes often bring the "Why?" questions – why me, why now? Almost as common are the "What? and How?" questions – What am I supposed to do? How am I supposed to go on?

I was contemplating such a change when these lyrics came on the radio – "Your world's not falling apart/ it's falling into place/ I'm on the throne/ stop holding on, and just be held."* God has a purpose behind what He allows in our lives. While the events might initially look random and seem like they're leading to destruction, He will arrange them in such a way that they work for our good. Because He's got it all under His perfect control, we can stop fighting Him and rest in His care.

And by the way, the good He's working on is to conform us into the image of Christ. So, don't fight Him – just be held.

"And we know that God causes all things to work together for good to those who love God, to those who are called according to His purpose. For those whom He foreknew, He also predestined to become conformed to the image of His Son." (Romans 8:28-29)

*"Just be Held," Casting Crowns

DAY 47 – LIFE-FILLED LIVING

She amazed me. She valiantly battled cancer for years, yet every time I saw her, she shared a genuine smile. Generally, she sat near the back of our sanctuary to make getting in and out a bit easier. But one Sunday near the end of her life, she made her way nearer the front, sitting one pew ahead of me.

At one point during the service, I looked up and caught her out of the corner of my eye. What I saw warmed my heart. While many others were simply listening, she was feverishly taking notes in the margins of her Bible! Why does one do that if they don't fully expect to come back to that portion of Scripture one day and review their notes?

When I asked her about it later, she said she took such notes because she never knew how God might use that particular Scripture in her life later. For instance, God may nudge her to use her notes in a letter to someone else to encourage them! Friends, she was within weeks of the end of her earthly journey, but she was still thinking of how God wanted to use her in the lives of others. I love it!

The reality is none of us knows how long we may have remaining. But I know this much: this victorious soul packed her days with life, and she inspired others to do the same. I'm reminded of a childhood prayer made very profound when one youngster "misspoke" it… "Now I lay me down to sleep. I pray the Lord my soul to keep. *If I should wake before I die*, I pray the Lord my soul to take."

Oh how we need to "wake" and be fully alive, before we die. Will you?

DAY 48 – IT'S EVERYWHERE!

You'd never know it by watching the news, but it's happening all over the globe.

It's occurring on every continent, in every country, and all over your community. Today, thousands of meals are being prepared for the mom and dad who just had a baby. Hams are being baked, casseroles put together, desserts made to share with the woman who just became a widow.

Over and over and over again, these and countless other examples of God's love are being manifested throughout His creation. Good is being done in His name. Love is being extended as He moves in the hearts of some to care for the hearts of others. And it's all done behind the scenes, without the spotlights or cameras. Why? Because God's love is poured out for the benefit of others, not for the attention of others.

Not only does God's love show up through the actions of His people, but He demonstrates it each day when the sun rises, when rain soaks the thirsty land, and when food and shelter are provided. Ultimately, the Father's love was poured out when His Son went to the cross.

The psalmist put it this way: "*The earth is full of the steadfast love of the Lord*" (Psalm 33:5, ESV).

His goodness and kindness are present everywhere, every day; it is steadfast – continuous, never ending. But we may need to look beyond the headlines if we're to see. What evidence of His love can you spot today? How can you help Him spread His love to others?

DAY 49 – FULLY OPEN

A woman named Lydia, from the city of Thyatira, a seller of purple fabrics, a worshiper of God, was listening; and the Lord opened her heart to respond to the things spoken by Paul. (Acts 16:14)

Lydia. Personally, I think it's a beautiful name. And objectively, what Lydia did in Acts 16 was undeniably beautiful!

We don't know a whole lot about her other than she was from Asia Minor, she specialized in purple fabric, and she worshipped God. But the thing I find most fascinating about her was that she *listened to* Paul. The original language suggests that Lydia arrived with the intention of *giving an audience* to him. She came with an open mind to hear what God might have to say to her.

The result? God opened her heart to respond. Isn't that awesome? As we open our minds and ears to hear God, He works within us, opening our hearts to respond. The Greek word for *opened* (*dianoigó*) means to *open fully by completing the process necessary to do so.* In other words, anything that's blocking the door of our heart from opening fully is removed.

We've all had situations in which we tried to open a physical door only to find that something is preventing it from swinging open. It could be a box, an old shoe, a chair – you name it, any number of things can get in the way. Not until the obstruction is removed will that door respond to our pushing.

Friends, sometimes the barrier to an open heart is our refusal to listen to what God has already told us. Do you want your heart to be responsive to our Lord? Then listen to Him.

DAY 50 – FEAR IS FUTILE

Once in a while, I come across a message that simply needs to be shared without much editorializing. Like so many of you, I struggle with various fears, so today I'd like to share the following words on the topic from Pastor Selwyn Hughes:

When Simon Peter stepped out of the boat and attempted to walk on the water to Jesus, he was afraid. "And beginning to sink he cried out 'Lord, save me!'" (Matthew 14:30). Fear makes you sink.

When Jesus healed the paralytic, His first word was, "Have courage, son," and His second, "Your sins are forgiven" (Matthew 9:2). When Jesus lifted the guilt, this lifted the fear which, in turn, lifted the paralysis.

When the disciples fell on their faces at the top of the Mount of Transfiguration, terrified because they had heard the voice of God, Jesus said: "Get up; don't be afraid" (Matthew 17:7). Fear puts you down; faith lifts you up.

The man who brought back the unused talent said: "I was afraid and went off and hid your talent in the ground" (Matthew 25:25). His life investment was in a hole in the ground! Fear did it.

Again, it was said of the disciples that they were gathered, "with the doors locked because of their fear of the Jews" (John 20:19). Fear always puts you behind closed doors; it causes you to become an ingrown person.

Joseph of Arimathea was "a disciple of Jesus – but secretly because of his fear of the Jews" (John 19:38). Fear always drives a person underground.

Look at the effects of fear mentioned above. It makes us sink, steals our courage, puts us down, paralyzes us, puts us behind closed doors, and drives us underground. No wonder the consistent message of Scripture is DO NOT FEAR. If God is for us, who indeed can be against us? (Romans 8:31)

<h1 style="text-align:center">DAY 51 – MOUNTAINS AND MOLE HILLS</h1>

The subject line of the email read, "Tell us how we did." Oh boy, how I wanted to tell them! The truth is – they'd messed up. It was one of those "ship to store" options and the retailer had sent me a message saying the item was ready for pickup. But when I got to the store to pick it up, it wasn't ready. Nor could they tell me when to expect it. Ugh.

On December 23rd, an extra trip to the store, not to mention the extra time it required, sure seemed like a pretty big deal. In fact, when the customer service survey arrived on December 27th, I still wanted to give them a small piece of my mind. But I was sick with the flu and just wasn't up to it. By the time I saw the email again days later, I just smiled and moved it to the recycle bin. The extra trip to the store didn't kill me, the gift was presented to the recipient and brought them much joy, and Christmas came and went just fine.

Isn't that the way it often goes with our problems? When they first crop up, they seem like such mountains to overcome. We may worry and fret about how to handle them, or we may become quickly angry because we're stressed at the time they arrive. I'm not downplaying the issues we have to face from time to time; I'm just suggesting that maybe we'd do well to allow a little time to pass so that we might gain a better perspective. Once we've sized up the situation a little better and taken some time to consult God about it, we'll be much better prepared to deal with it.

Mountains are hard to climb – mole hills not so much. Make sure you've given yourself the needed time to tell which you're dealing with!

Whoever is patient has great understanding, but one who is quick-tempered displays folly. (Proverbs 14:29)

It's one of the most fascinating stories in the Old Testament. I just love the way Elijah takes on the priests of Baal and kicks some false-god fanny! If you're not familiar with it, I encourage you to read the whole account in 1 Kings 18.

In short, Elijah (a prophet of the true God) sets up a challenge between Yahweh and the false god Baal. Why? – Because the people of Israel had fallen away and were following Baal. As the showdown was being set up, Elijah assembled all the people and asked them a question that I believe God continues to ask us today:

> *How long will you waver between two opinions? If
> the Lord is God, follow Him; but if Baal is God, follow him.*
> (1 Kings 18:21)

Elijah paints a pretty simple picture for us. In this world, there is God, and there's not God (everything else); we're to choose which we will follow. The original wording implies that the people were *limping along* or *hesitating* as if they were unsure of their footing. Such vacillation slows us down and prevents us from following quickly and confidently.

I find the Hebrews' answer very telling: "…*the people said nothing*" (v.21). There simply were no words to explain how the children of God had left Him in deference to statues made of wood, idols to whom they were sacrificing their own children (Jeremiah 19:5). It was too hard to explain – they didn't even try.

Friends, the world continues to offer the same two opinions – God, and all things not God. As this story warns us, if we don't follow Him closely, we'll waver and perhaps wander much farther away than we can imagine. Don't waver – cling to Christ.

DAY 53 – EVEN THERE

One of the recurring themes throughout the life of Joseph was that "the Lord was with him." In fact, that phrase appears about half a dozen times just in Genesis 39 alone.

I am particularly curious about the circumstances during which Scripture says God remained by Joseph's side. When his brothers sold him into slavery, the Lord was with him. When Joseph rose within the house of Potiphar, the Lord was with him. When Joseph was falsely accused and thrown into prison, the Lord was with him. When he became Pharaoh's second in command throughout all of Egypt, the Lord was with him.

During the mountain top moments and every valley in between, God stayed faithfully beside Joseph, and Joseph remained faithful to God. I guess there's nothing surprising there. But what I want us to be reminded of today is that even while walking closely with God, Joseph was allowed to be grossly mistreated by his brothers, severely tempted by Potiphar's wife, falsely accused of assault, and wrongfully imprisoned.

Being in right relationship with God does not make us immune to the trials of this world. God did not promise us a journey free of difficulty – in fact, He promised just the opposite when He said that in this world we would have troubles (John 16:33).

No, Christ doesn't protect us from everything, but He does promise to walk by our sides as we go through whatever He allows.

> *But while Joseph was there in the prison, the Lord was with him.* (Genesis 39:20-21)

DAY 54 – CAN'T AFFORD

Back in the day when door-to-door sales were popular, the story was told of a clever salesman who closed hundreds of sales with this line:

> *Let me show you something several of your neighbors said you couldn't afford!*

It never gets old to me – I laugh every time I read it! However, it's only funny because there's an element of truth involved. I shudder to look around my home and see the many things I have purchased for no real reason.

Jesus knows our needs and has promised to meet them. However, the "need" to impress, or to keep up with, our neighbors isn't one of them. In fact, He cautioned against even trying. Instead, He said to focus on His Kingdom and righteousness – if we'll do so, every other thing we need will somehow fall into its proper place.

Instead of seeking your neighbor's approval, seek your Savior's Kingdom and His righteousness – we can't afford not to.

> *But seek first his kingdom and his righteousness, and all these things will be given to you as well.* (Matthew 6:33)

DAY 55 – LOVED, LOVE, LOVABLE

Benjamin Franklin once stated, "If you would be loved, love, and be lovable." I'm no expert in the field, but I would guess that to be loved is among man's greatest needs. Simply put, we all long to be loved.

Ultimately, that deep need can be met only through a personal relationship with Christ. However, Franklin's words include a lot of wisdom for our human relationships as well. If you want to be given love, give love. If you want to receive love, be easy to love.

This is not intended to set up a conditional system for giving and receiving love (although human nature will try to make it into one). As followers of Christ, we're to give love regardless of how loving or lovable the other person is. However, when it comes to receiving love, why not make it as easy on the other person as possible?

Lord, as the God who is love, help us give our love freely, and to make it easy for others to love us, as well.

> *Now about your love for one another we do not need to write to you, for you yourselves have been taught by God to love each other. (1 Thessalonians 4:9)*

DAY 56 – ON HOLD

I recently read an article by an expert in the field of customer service, who wrote that the average caller will begin to experience (and express) frustration after being kept on hold for twenty seconds – twenty seconds! If handled well by the phone agent, a caller might tolerate a hold time of "up to one full minute."

Believe me, I don't like to be kept on hold either, but I also spent more than twenty years in a pharmaceutical call center trying to provide answers to clinical and technical questions about hundreds of medications. Sometimes, I knew the answers off the top of my head, but frequently I didn't know, and needed time to find out before responding. Let me tell you, when you're on the other side of the phone, those same twenty to sixty seconds fly by and are not nearly enough time to conduct a thorough search.

My point is simply this – when it comes to "hold time," perspective is everything. To us here on earth, the time we are forced to wait for answers or endure difficult circumstances feels like an eternity. However, to the One who holds all the answers in eternity, it is nothing at all.

The next time God seems to have you "on hold," remember He is simply waiting for the perfect time to end your burden or provide the answer you've been seeking. Trust Him and try to wait patiently.

> *But do not overlook this one fact, beloved, that with the Lord one day is as a thousand years, and a thousand years as one day.* (2 Peter 3:8)

DAY 57 – GREAT SERVICE

While Martin Luther King, Jr. lived and died a little before my time, I find many of his truths to be timeless – primarily because they align so well with Scripture. Here is one that really stood out to me:

> *Everybody can be great…because anybody can serve. You don't have to have a college degree to serve. You don't have to make your subject and verb agree to serve. You only need a heart full of grace. A soul generated by love.*

King understood something that many of us seem to forget – true greatness is achieved not by higher education, career advancement, possessions, or earning potential. God's path to greatness is paved with service that stems from a heart of grace and love for others.

Christ put it in the simplest terms imaginable: "*The greatest among you shall be your servant*" (Matthew 23:11). As He reminded His disciples, Jesus came not to be served, but to serve others (Mark 10:45).

Friends, we truly can all be "great" – the key is serving others.

If most of us had a Bible institute and/or a Christian publishing house named after us, we might have trouble fitting our head through the door! Not so with evangelist Dwight L. Moody.

Moody was an uneducated yet incredibly gifted man when he began preaching in Birmingham, England. After listening to Moody preach and seeing the incredible results of his ministry, Dr. R.W. Dale, a well-respected theologian of the same era, wrote, "I told Mr. Moody that the work was most plainly of God, for I could see no real relation between him and what he had done. Moody laughed cheerily and said, 'I should be very sorry if it were otherwise.'"

Wow – what a countercultural response! "I'd be sorry if these excellent results were of my own doing. I'd much rather God be active and given Him all the credit." Moody was completely willing for God to receive all the praise for the results coming from the work in which he participated. There was no defensiveness on Moody's part. No desire for fame, applause, or recognition. Men were hearing the message of forgiveness, and God's Spirit was causing them to respond to that message. That's ALL that mattered to Moody. That humility is probably why we find Bible colleges and publication houses in Moody's name today.

If we see results from our efforts, may we be as happy as Moody was for others to state that the work is plainly of God! In fact, may we be very sorry if it were otherwise.

> *I planted, Apollos watered, but God gave the growth.* (1 Corinthians 3:6, ESV)

DAY 59 – DABBLE OR DIVE?

*I pray that your partnership with us in the faith may be
effective in deepening your understanding of every good
thing we share for the sake of Christ.* (Philemon 1:6)

Dabbling. That's how I'd describe my involvement in many
activities. I dabble at the piano. I dabble at gardening. I dabble
at bird watching, crossword puzzles, and photography. I enjoy
each for a while and then move on to other interests. As a result, I
haven't really mastered any of them.

In some ways, I believe many of us dabble at our faith. We give it
some attention from time to time, but we never really give it our
all. As a result, we feel somewhat unsatisfied or disappointed with
"the whole church/religion/faith thing." I understand, because I've
been there myself.

If that's your experience, I encourage you to carefully consider
Paul's words above. In them I believe is a secret to deep and rich
fulfillment in Christ. Instead of merely participating in things of the
faith from time to time, Paul tells us to become *partners* in it.
Implied in the word are the ideas of *diving in and becoming fully
involved in the activities and the outcomes.* It's not a passing
interest, but a vested interest.

Notice what the result will be if we'll dive in – a deeper knowledge
of all that is truly ours in Christ. In other words, the more we roll
up our sleeves and serve Christ alongside others, the more we'll
appreciate the One we serve.

Are you feeling like an "outsider looking in" at church? Finding
your relationship with Christ a bit stale? Perhaps the key to
appreciating your life of faith is to stop dabbling in it and simply
dive into the deep end instead!

DAY 60 – GAINING BY ABSTAINING

If you're like me, you probably learned only half the truth. As a child I thought that to *abstain* from anything was to go completely without it – to give something up totally, at least for a period of time.

That's not wrong – it's just incomplete. The Greek word used in Scripture for *abstain* is formed by two smaller words that literally mean *to have one thing by letting go of another*. The actual focus in abstinence is NOT on what is given up, but upon what is GAINED by doing so!

Take for example Paul's instructions below regarding immoral sexual activity.

> *It is God's will that you should be sanctified: that you should avoid sexual immorality; that each of you should learn to control your own body in a way that is holy and honorable…* (1 Thessalonians 4:3-4)

Certainly the followers of Christ were to forego sex outside of marriage. However, to focus solely on what they were "giving up" was only part of the story. When Scripture tells us to give something up, it generally provides a better alternative. In the passage above, the advantages gained while letting go of immorality are self-control, holiness, and honor. May we never overlook God's better alternatives.

Think about the things God may have asked you to do without. Now ask Him to show you all you'll gain by doing so.

DAY 61 – EMPTIED AND FILLED

More often than not, I do NOT get this right, so please don't think I'm tooting my own horn – I'm not! But recently, I was spending time with an old friend and it became apparent they had come into hard times financially. It didn't matter how they got there; the only thing of importance was that there was a need.

Without a thought, I took out my wallet and handed over everything I had with me. No, it wasn't enough to make a dent in the overall need, but it was good for both of us – good for me to give all I had and good for them to humbly accept.

Later, as I drove home, the words of Proverbs 3 came to mind. *"Do not withhold good from those to whom it is due, when it is in your power to do it. Do not say to your neighbor, 'Go, and come again, tomorrow I will give it'— when you have it with you"* (vv.27-28). How often in the past have I said, "I need to pray about it," when in reality all I wanted was time to find a reason to say "no"?

As I got home, I realized that sometimes – despite my fears to the contrary – an empty wallet can actually be associated with a very full heart.

If the need is now and you have the means to meet the need now – go for it! You won't regret it.

DAY 62 – LOVIN' OUR WORK

Labor Day, the first Monday of September, is set aside to pay tribute to the achievements of the American worker. It had its origins in the labor movement of the late 19th century and was first declared a federal holiday by President Grover Cleveland in 1894.

Perhaps contrary to the belief of many, work has always been a part of the human experience to be celebrated. In fact, it began with Adam. *"The Lord God took the man and put him in the Garden of Eden **to work it** and take care of it"* (Genesis 2:15, emphasis added). And friends, that assignment of work was given to Adam BEFORE the fall. God blessed man with work to expand his horizons, help occupy his time, and to experience accomplishment. Only after the fall did work become toilsome and a heavy burden (Genesis 3:17).

Solomon frequently commanded men to work and enjoy work's benefits. Listen to just one example: *"when God gives someone wealth and possessions, and the ability to enjoy them, to accept their lot and be happy in their toil–this is a gift of God"* (Ecclesiastes 5:19).

Work, as well the ability to enjoy our lot in life, are gifts from God. When we see Him as the Giver of our work, the result is great joy. However, work devoid of God is frequently just a great toil. What difference might it make if you began seeing your work as a gift from God?

DAY 63 – SOWING AND GROWING

"Nothing sown, nothing grown."

The phrase appeared as part of a warning that Moses gave to Israel. If they failed to follow God's commands, their children would inherit a land where no seed was sown and no plant would sprout (Deuteronomy 29:22-23).

While I read the passage, my mind kept repeating that four-word rhyme – "nothing sown, nothing grown." I hate to admit it, but the warning still applies today. If we don't plant, water, fertilize, and weed in the next generation, we won't see anything we want growing there.

But if that's true, then the reverse must also be true – "something sown, something grown"! If the failure to sow seeds prevents the next crop from growing, then faithfully sowing will lead to a harvest. One spring, I began preparing my garden. I manually turned the soil with my grandfather's old shovel. But if I didn't take the next step of planting seed, I couldn't expect to see anything grow but weeds.

But if I sowed carrot seeds, I could expect to reap carrots. If I planted potatoes, potatoes would grow. Likewise, if we sow seeds of righteousness, we can expect righteousness to grow.

"Nothing sown, nothing grown." "Something sown, something grown." What seeds are you planting?

> *For as the soil makes the sprout come up and a garden causes seeds to grow, so the Sovereign Lord will make righteousness and praise spring up before all nations.* (Isaiah 61:11)

DAY 64 – THE BURDEN AND THE LOAD

No one is useless in this world who lightens the burdens of another.
-Charles Dickens

My late sister used to say, "A joy shared is twice the joy. A burden shared is half the burden." Oh, how we need burden-bearers today!

To the Christians in Galatia, Paul wrote:

> *Carry each other's burdens, and in this way you will fulfill the law of Christ. (6:2)*

Yet a few verses later, Paul said "*each one should carry their own load*" (6:5). So which is it, Paul? In short, it's both. The key to this apparent contradiction is understanding the difference between a LOAD (for which we are personally responsible) and a BURDEN (which can be shared).

Load in verse 5 is from the Greek *phortion* – which means *a responsibility which must be carried by the individual, i.e. something personal that cannot be shifted to someone else.* For example, I am responsible for my mortgage, to fulfill the duties of my job, to raise and discipline my children, and so on. These are MY responsibilities – the load I'm expected to carry daily.

Burden in verse 2 is from a different word, *baros,* which means *weight.* Burdens are the extra, unexpected challenges in life (above and beyond the load described above) that bring additional difficulty to someone's journey. Perhaps a job loss makes it impossible to make the mortgage payment for a month – fellow Christians can step in and help lift some of that burden. Or perhaps a couple with a special needs child requires help on occasion so they can get out of the house for a date.

The mortgage and the children remain the LOAD of the original bearers to carry, but the special circumstances become the responsibility of the church to share.

Are you faithfully carrying your personal load? Are you willing to help carry your brother's or sister's excessive burdens?

DAY 65 – PLAGUES, PAIN, AND PURPOSE

I recently taught a class on the plagues in Exodus. Ultimately the plagues led the Israelites out of slavery in Egypt, yet there was an even bigger purpose behind them. Over and over, Moses recorded for us the Lord's purpose. And as the plagues "crescendoed" in severity, God expanded His purpose. What was that purpose? That the Lord would be known.

First, God showed His power to Pharaoh and his magicians alone so that they might know that the Egyptian gods were no gods at all (Exodus 7). Next, God wanted all of Egypt to know Him through the plagues He brought (8:22). But that, too, was not enough. Therefore God performed further plagues so that His name might become known throughout the whole earth (9:14). But God was not content for only one generation to know Him, so He brought the final plagues so that Israel would tell their children and grandchildren about Him (10:2). God's glorious plan was for all people in all generations to come to know Him.

To *know* God in the book of Exodus was to *experience* Him, to perceive with all of one's senses that "He is," and to acknowledge Him for who He is. As a result, God's hope was that all would submit to Him and be saved through faith in Him.

Yes, people suffered during the plagues. Each day God delayed their release, the Israelites remained in cruel slavery. The Egyptians felt the brunt of the hail, locusts, and boils, and so on. But God had a purpose in His plagues and in their pain – that He might be known.

Friends, perhaps you're suffering today. If so, remember that God never wastes a hurt – He has a purpose in the pain He allows. Look for ways Christ may become known through you as you endure your trials.

> *The Egyptians shall know that I am the Lord, when I stretch out my hand against Egypt and bring out the people of Israel from among them. (Exodus 7:5)*

DAY 66 – KEYS

It was past time for my kids to have house keys of their own, so I stopped by one of the local stores and had a couple made. As I stood at the counter, I was overwhelmed by the number of options available. There were Disney Princesses, ladybugs, monkeys, M&M's, and a host of others. I chose a key for each girl and handed them to the key-making guy.

The employee stood there for a moment and looked at me like I had two heads before finally concluding that I just wasn't "getting it." Apparently, he needed the original to get started and I was still holding it!

As the machine ground away, I thought about the similarities that existed between Christians and keys. We come in a variety of shapes, sizes, and colors. Our personalities, looks, and abilities may all differ. However, if we're going to be effective, there must be a likeness to the Original.

Like with those keys, everything about us that is not of the Master must be ground away. Only when we resemble our Father in heaven will the grinding process be completed. The process may be painful, but it's necessary – so try not to fight it. Remember, He has a purpose for every second spent in the grinder.

> *...we all are being transformed into His image with ever-increasing glory...* (2 Corinthians 3:18).

DAY 67 – A CHEERFUL LOOK

A cheerful look brings joy to the heart (Proverbs 15:30).

Sometimes, it's the simple things that can make the biggest difference. Most of us want joy in our hearts, and we'd like to bring joy to others too if we can. The proverb above gives us a means of accomplishing both, but the question then becomes, "What's a cheerful look?"

At first glance, it may appear like we ought to simply smile more frequently – and, research actually supports that a smile definitely lifts the spirits (ours and others). But the original language takes us deeper than a smile on the surface. *Bright eyes gladden the heart* is how the original would read. You see, while others may smile at us when we pass, their eyes will often tell a different story. Our eyes just aren't very good liars!

As one commentator explained, "The beaming glance that shows a pure, happy mind and a friendly disposition rejoices the heart of him on whom it is turned." There is something infectious in the joyful look of a genuinely happy individual, which has a cheering effect upon those who observe it. That's the impact we can have on others.

But the proverb also hints at how to obtain that joy ourselves. The wording also very much teaches that what we choose to focus on impacts our outlook. When the Old Testament was translated from Hebrew into Greek, the proverb was worded this way: *"The eye that sees what is good rejoices the heart."* Read in this manner, it conjures up Paul's encouragement to focus on whatever is pure, good, lovely, praiseworthy, and such (Philippians 4:8).

Want to be a well of joy? Focus your eyes on whatever is good, and then let your eyes reflect that joy to others. Oh, and smile more!

Like many of you, I enjoy finding a good deal. After deciding to purchase something, I often like the "hunt" of finding the best price.

When I ran my business, I tried to negotiate the best deals possible, and when I file my taxes I try to avoid paying more than I must. It's good, common sense in my mind.

So when the idea of intentionally leaving the best deal on the table for the benefit of other people surfaces, it runs contrary to human nature. Yet God frequently tells us to provide for others, which almost always comes at a personal cost. For instance, in Deuteronomy, the Israelites were told:

> *When you harvest the grapes in your vineyard, do not go over the vines again. Leave what remains for the foreigner, the fatherless and the widow. Remember that you were slaves in Egypt. That is why I command you to do this. (24:21-22)*

In other words, don't walk your fields even a second time to collect everything you can for yourself. Instead, intentionally leave some behind to share. I'm sure that was a difficult proposition then too. It forced them to stretch their faith – would God provide for them or not? The truth is, that's the same question we face when we give today as well. But as verse 22 tells us, God has consistently demonstrated His faithful provision for His children.

I don't pretend to know your financial situation today, and I'd never stick my nose in where it doesn't belong – but I firmly believe God still desires for His people to be sensitive toward the needs of others, and He still wants us to regularly set aside some of what we have for that purpose.

How might you set aside some grapes to share today?

DAY 69 – MORE OF YOU

It was our thirtieth wedding anniversary. As I reflected on three decades of married life, I was grateful for the faithfulness of my wife and our God.

It's definitely been a rollercoaster of a ride! There have been long periods of waiting. Slow, steep climbs to the top of hills we never thought we'd conquer. Terrifying plunges into dark, deep valleys. Confusing times of not knowing what was around the bend. Twists and turns that jerked us around and made us sick. Yet somehow after thirty laps around, we smile and say, "What a ride – Let's do it again!"

Over the course of thirty years, one racks up a collection of memories. Many joys, some heartaches, a few regrets. Looking back, my regrets have all stemmed from one root – failing to love my wife and daughters as Christ loved His church. As I type, I'm hearing these words from Wayne Watson's song, "More of You":

> All she really needs from me, is more of You/
> More understanding, more tenderness/
> A love that goes beyond my humanness/
> That's all she really needs from me/
> Is more of You, more of You.

Looking ahead, I know that more of Christ along with less of the selfish little stinker that is Dave equals better relationships.

Do you want to strengthen your relationships? Then give to others more of Christ and less of you.

> *Husbands, love your wives, just as Christ loved the church and gave himself up for her. (Ephesians 5:25)*

DAY 70 – BE BRAVE

From the looks of it, nearly each of the 18,972 seats was filled. On stage were many of Christian music's biggest names. The Winter Jam concert is a five- to seven-hour ordeal, and for the first time, Amanda wanted to attend.

For those who don't know, Amanda's neurological system makes her VERY sensitive to loud noises and chaotic crowds. A dozen family members in one house used to be too much for her. So when she wanted to go to THIS concert, I was apprehensive. Having attended Winter Jam previously, I feared she was underestimating how overwhelming the event would be.

However, her response to my concerns convinced me we had to try. Here were her well-thought-out words:

> *I know it will be overwhelming, Dad – but I want to be brave. I'm tired of being afraid.*

Enough said. To tell you the truth, I was a bit afraid too – for her, for my wife, for myself. But if she was willing to face over 5 hours of nearly 19,000 screaming fans, then how could I say no? So we gathered our ear plugs, said our prayers, and made arrangements to have two vehicles at the venue "just in case." But just in case never came. For the next five hours I watched a young woman simply enjoy her favorite artists singing some of her favorite songs. For her bravery, she was even invited backstage to meet Hollyn, one of the performers!

Friends, we never envisioned this day. We never thought Amanda would WANT to do such a thing, and we never thought she COULD do such a thing. But she did! And it happened because Amanda trusted God to help her be brave in the face of her fears. Do I write to boast about Amanda? Yes, at least a little bit! But, I also boast about our God who helps us be brave. As Paul wrote to Timothy, God has given us a Spirit of boldness and power, not fear (2 Timothy 1:7).

God's Spirit gives you what you need to face your fears – so be brave!

> *For the Spirit God gave us does not make us timid, but gives us power, love and self-discipline.* (2 Timothy 1:7)

DAY 71 – SEMPER GUMBY

I have a dear friend I've had since grade school. We both have daughters who went to college at the same time. While mine only went two hours away to the relative safety of a small, private university, hers went half-way across the country to become a West Point cadet.

That fall, my friend introduced me to the concept of "Semper Gumby" – a play on the Marine Corp's slogan "Semper Fi," meaning "Always Faithful." To military families, "Semper Gumby" means "Always Flexible." It serves as a reminder that a soldier's orders can (and often do) change without notice. Unfortunately, these changes aren't run past the parents for their approval. No, the immediate need of the branch comes first, and Mom and Dad are forced to relinquish any sense of control and simply let go. As they've learned, flexibility is absolutely essential for surviving in the military, and it has become a way of life for their entire family.

Knowing they miss their daughter a great deal, I frequently ask about her. After sharing a few details, it is not unusual for the eyes of this dedicated parent to well up with tears before she turns them off and with great resolve says, "Semper Gumby!"

I can't possibly understand all that those words mean when she says them. However, for me, Semper Gumby means that things aren't going the way I would have chosen, and frankly, I feel scared and completely out of control. If we're honest, that's the reality with a great deal of life – things often don't go as we'd like, and we have little control over them. When that's the case, what is to be our response? Do we fret and worry, driving ourselves and those around us a bit crazy? Or, in faith, do we place our cares into the hands of our Heavenly Father, keep our knees flexed, and willingly move however He directs?

Feeling scared and out of control? Remember, Semper Gumby.

For you, O Lord, are my hope and my trust. (Psalm 71:5)

I bet it's happened to you as well. You're driving along when someone in the car suddenly shouts, "Wait, I left something at the house!" Immediately, many calculations fly through your mind: How important is the forgotten item? Do we have time to return home and still reach our destination on time? But perhaps most importantly, how far have we gone?

Obviously, the further from home you've traveled, the less likely you are to turn around and retrieve whatever was left behind. At some point, the distance between you and "it" becomes so great that it's futile to go back.

It's interesting to me that when David wrote about the forgiveness of God he chose to illustrate it with a map. This man, who admittedly had committed some major offenses against God, was the one who wrote this: "*as far as the east is from the west, so far does He remove our transgressions from us*" (Psalm 103:12). David's hope was to demonstrate the limitless distance that separates a child of God from their confessed and forgiven sins. They are removed an infinite number of miles, never to return.

Friends, if that's true (and it is), don't you think it's pointless to continue to carry the baggage of those sins any longer? They are gone. You could drive forever and ever, and you would never encounter them again – so don't even try. Besides, you'll never reach the destinations Christ has for you if you're constantly turning around. Instead, thank God for His forgiveness, forget about what lies behind, focus on what lies ahead, and then enjoy the journey!

DAY 73 – GIVEN, NOT TAKEN

All things were created by Him, and apart from Him not one thing was created that has been created. (John 1:3, NET)

John's gospel is pretty clear on the topic – Jesus was involved in the creation of ALL things. Not one thing was made without His involvement. That truth took on a new meaning for me one Good Friday and Resurrection Sunday.

As Max Lucado once wrote: "Jesus planned His own sacrifice. Jesus intentionally planted the tree from which His cross would be carved. He willingly placed the iron ore in the heart of the earth from which the nails would be cast. He voluntarily placed Judas in the womb of a woman. He didn't have to do it – but He did."

Christ's death was not a tragic accident. He wasn't caught in the wrong place at the wrong time or the victim of unfortunate circumstances. Far from it. Jesus knew exactly when Pilate and Herod were born. He knew every hair on every head of every Pharisee who would later condemn Him. He formed the hands of the Roman soldiers who held the whip and hammered the nails. He grew the thorns that would one day form His only earthly crown.

It's no wonder then that Jesus Himself would say this about His own death: "*No man takes my life from me, I willingly lay it down*" (John 10:18).

Willingly…knowingly…and all for you. Spend some time today to thank Him that His life was given, not taken.

DAY 74 – HANGING ON AND LETTING GO

It doesn't take a lot of strength to hang on. It takes a lot of strength to let go.
-JC Watts

Boy, do these words ring true to my ears. I am the epitome of a "hanger-on." One look around my home tells everyone that I love to cling to old stuff. Our kitchen still has its original wallpaper and appliances thirty years after we moved in. Our van has more than 245,000 miles; our daughters' first dollhouses are still in the basement. On and on I could go, but you get the idea.

Why? Why do we hold on to something that has run its course? Why do we not throw away worn-out things? Why do we cling to the lifeless corpses of dead jobs or unhealthy relationships? Why do we return to old wells even if the water is stale or even poisonous to us?

Honestly, I think Watts is correct – we lack the strength to let go of what is known. Our current circumstances may be crummy, but they're at least ours! And we're generally much more comfortable with what is known (even if it's unpleasant) than with taking a leap of faith into the unknown. Yet Scripture tells us that without faith, it is impossible to please God – not difficult , IMPOSSIBLE (Hebrews 11:6).

Perhaps that's why one of Paul's frequent prayers for his readers was that they would be strengthened in their faith. Only faith gives us the strength to let go of the past and fully embrace the future.

Still holding on to something you know God would have you give up? If so, ask Christ to give you the faith and strength necessary to let go.

*So then, just as you received Christ Jesus as
Lord, continue to live your lives in him, rooted and built up
in him, strengthened in the faith as you were taught, and
overflowing with thankfulness. (Colossians 2:6-7)*

DAY 75 – GARAGE OR SIDEWALK?

I was getting frustrated. Our neighborhood was hosting its first
community-wide garage sale. For a week we sorted through our
belongings and prepared our garage for the big event.

Friday morning arrived, but shoppers did not. More often than not,
all we got were cars slowing down to take a brief look before
driving down the street and stopping at another sale. As they
rolled past I wanted to yell, "Hey – my junk (I mean treasure) is as
good as theirs – why not stop here?"

As Day One of the sale ended, I walked up the street to one of the
busier homes and asked what their "secret" was. My neighbor
looked toward my home and said, "Dave, all your stuff is inside
your garage – nobody can see what you have." I hadn't even
thought of it. Because of the weather forecast, I left most of our
treasure inside in case of rain. As a result, nobody could see what
was there.

I determined that the next day would be different. On Day Two, I
would not keep my treasure hidden safe within the walls of my
garage. Instead, it was going to be littering my driveway for all to
view. Some may still have walked past, not interested in what I
had to share. But they would ALL at least be exposed!

Friends – the same is true of the real treasure we have inside us.
People will not have the opportunity to respond to the gospel if
they don't see it. We must live the gospel "out loud" – not keep it
safely hidden within the walls of our heart's garage.

Is your faith an "inside the garage" or an "out on the driveway"
thing? Take a chance; let it cover your "driveway!" Many may
walk by without interest – but if even one shows curiosity, isn't it
worth it?

> *No one lights a lamp and hides it in a clay jar or puts it
> under a bed. Instead, they put it on a stand, so that those
> who come in can see the light.* (Luke 8:16)

DAY 76 – WEAKNESS WELCOME

Author Henri Nouwen once wrote, "When we honestly ask ourselves which people in our lives mean the most to us, we often find that it is those who, instead of giving advice, solutions, or cures, have chosen rather to share our pain and touch our wounds with a warm and tender hand." No wonder he would conclude that, "We minister above all with our weakness."

Certainly we can teach, lead, and give to others from positions of strength. But to truly minister to the hurting, we must be willing to set aside appearances of having it all together and expose our weakness. For it is generally in our moments of weakness that we first experience the comforting hand of God ourselves. It is during those dark and lonely hours, when our hearts were broken and dreams dashed, that we discovered that God does indeed dwell among the contrite and lowly to revive our hearts and spirits (Isaiah 57:15).

Once we have experienced the comfort, hope, and healing from God in our lives, we can begin to share that comfort with others (2 Corinthians 1:3-4). But we must allow it to be used and not hide it from others once the immediacy of the moment has passed. As difficult as it may be for us to believe, our hurt and brokenness may be the very tools God wants to use to minister to others.

As Philip Yancey notes, we need to remember that "we are pilgrims progressing, not pilgrims arrived. We are fellow travelers, not professional guides. The uncommitted respond best to someone who leads from weakness rather than one who appears to have it all together."

If His strength is perfect in our weakness, shouldn't we be willing to remain weak so others may find that Christ is strong and sufficient?

DAY 77 – BIRDS OF A DIFFERENT FEATHER

My beloved Uncle Charlie recently gave me a new bird feeder, and I've been enjoying hours on my porch watching the various species come and go. At one point, I looked up to see quite the collection on (and under) the feeder. There was a male and a female cardinal, a white-crowned sparrow, a house sparrow, mourning doves, grackles, robins, and an otherwise unidentifiable finch! Or was it a chickadee?   I'm still learning.

As I sat quietly and smiled, I couldn't help but wonder if that is the joy God experiences when His children – red or yellow, black or white – gather together in unity. Each bird was unique in its color, song, and behavior, but all were comfortable in one another's presence. Unfortunately, however, it didn't last forever. It wasn't long before a bully blue jay crashed the scene and scattered the flock.   But it was beautiful while it lasted.

That's the thing about genuine unity – it's altogether rare and beautiful, but it's also fragile. What can you do to promote unity in the groups to which you belong?

> *How good and pleasant it is when God's people live together in unity!* (Psalm 133:1)

DAY 78 – IN TUNE

The conversation began with my daughter giving me an idea for a Christmas gift – she wanted the piano tuned. We've had it in our basement since we moved in (in 1991), and I can't remember ever having it tuned, so I'm sure it was WAY overdue.

However, my first response was, "But it sounds fine to me." In her wisdom, Amy didn't argue with me; she just opened YouTube and played a video of a song on her phone as she played along on the piano. They were supposed to be in the same key. But the clash was horrific – it turns out the piano was about a half-step flat. When played by itself, it sounded fine. But when played in concert with another instrument – well, you had better have had earplugs!

What's true for my out-of-tune piano can easily be true of people as well. In our tendency toward isolation, we may think we "sound good" by ourselves, while the whole time we're sorely out of tune with God and/or His people. One of the reasons Scripture tells us not to give up meeting together (Hebrews 10:25) is so that we remain "in tune" with God and with the rest of His "choir."

Ultimately, however, it is Christ to whom we want to be most closely aligned. Only when we each tune our lives to Him can we be sure we will live in harmony with God and others. Take an honest look at your life – is it time for a tune up?

...be conformed to the image of his Son... (Romans 8:29)

DAY 79 – 22ND STREET

It was late November in northeast Kansas, and our travel home was being threatened by weather. Surprisingly, however, it wasn't sleet or snow. Just as we crossed the Missouri River the tornado sirens began blaring! The winds were so strong atop the Pony Express Bridge I feared the van might be thrown into the river below. I tried to remain calm for the others, but I was pretty freaked out. We could barely see anything, we were ninety miles from home, and we knew nobody in St. Joe, Missouri. Yet the worst place to be during a tornado is in a car, so I began looking for a place to exit – FAST!

Instinctively, I took the first exit we came to – 22nd Street – and looked for a house with a light on inside. To this day, I don't remember how we ended up where we did, but the next thing I knew I was ringing the doorbell of complete strangers, asking if my family could ride out the storm with them. Without hesitation they waved us into their basement, where we waited for the "all clear."

During the wait, we learned this couple had only answered the door because they thought it might have been their teenage son ringing the bell. We quickly learned that they were a Christian family and they kindly prayed with us as they sent us on our way.

From that day to this, the 22nd Street Exit in St. Joseph, Missouri serves as a reminder of God's provision. When everything looked bleak, God provided a light for us to follow and a refuge from the storm. And He did so through other Christians who were willing to take some frightened strangers into their home.

What reminders of God's provision do you have? Would you open your door in a similar situation? Why or why not?

> *For in the day of trouble he will keep me safe in his dwelling; he will hide me in the shelter of his sacred tent and set me high upon a rock.* (Psalm 27:5)

DAY 80 – WANDERINGS, WOUNDS, WORSHIP

You Yourself have recorded my wanderings. Put my tears in Your bottle. Are they not in Your records? Then my enemies will retreat on the day when I call. This I know: God is for me. (Psalm 56:8-9, HCSB)

It's a song of intimate praise between a would-be king and his God. What makes these words even more amazing is the context in which David wrote them. Above this chapter, my Bible adds, "Of David. When the Philistines seized him in Gath."

David was on the run from Saul when he was captured by Israel's mortal enemy. He definitely fell out of the frying pan and directly into the fire! *Wanderings* here means *the aimless travels of a fugitive.* Some translations render it *misery.*

David was miserably alone, on the run, scared, and heartbroken from leaving his wife, his mentor, his best friend, his country, and his family. If there was ever a time for shedding tears, this was it.

I believe there are several lessons for us here. First, God is intimately aware of our **wanderings**. He knows our comings and goings. We may feel alone, but we're not – God is constantly present. Second, God is intimately aware of our **wounds**. He sees each heartache; He's aware of each injustice; He collects every tear. He even keeps a written record of them.

But perhaps the most amazing truth from this passage is David's conclusion. Despite the paths he was forced to travel and the deep wounds God allowed, David still clung to the truth that God was for him! And if that was true (and it was), then so was David's next conclusion in verse 11 – if God was for him, what could man do to him?

Friends, even when God allows seasons of aimless wandering and frequent wounds, He is still FOR US – and He is worthy of our worship. Never forget it!

DAY 81 – MISERABLE Scrooge

While it was only early November, my older daughter wanted to watch a version of Dicken's *A Christmas Carol*. Not very far into it, I found myself shaking my head at many of Scrooge's thoughtless antics. At one point I literally said, "You're just a miserable ol' miser, buddy."

Later, I couldn't shake how closely related our English word *miser* is to *misery* and *miserable*. My curiosity compelled me to investigate a bit, and sure enough, *miser* comes from a Latin word that means *miserable* or *wretched*.

I can't be too tough on Ebenezer, though, because I have some Scrooge DNA in my bloodstream too. I've gotten better over time, but I know I'm still prone to being miserly – holding too tightly to the things I consider "mine." However, when I hoard things to myself, I admit that I end up kind of miserable. Ironically, there is a sort of misery that accompanies my selfishness. In contrast, the times I've responded to others with generosity (of either time or money) have been marked by an incredible sense of joy and fulfillment.

So, if joy and fulfillment accompany giving and misery accompanies selfishness, why do I so often choose the latter? If I'm honest, it's because I fear that God won't supply my own need when that time rolls around. Silly, I know, but true.

In a sense, giving is an exercise in faith. Little should we be surprised, then, that anytime we act in faith, God is pleased and we are filled with joy. He loves a cheerful giver – perhaps, in part, because cheerful giving demonstrates faith in Him.

> *Each one must do just as he has purposed in his heart, not grudgingly or under compulsion, for God loves a cheerful giver.* (2 Corinthians 9:7)

DAY 82 – AMAZING FAITH

While Jesus walked the earth, He was often amazed by the faith He witnessed in those He encountered. Unfortunately, that amazement generally came in response to the **lack of** faith demonstrated by those closest to Him.

For example, in His hometown, Jesus refused to perform miracles because of their lack of faith (Matthew 13:57-58). Even His disciples, who saw Christ perform many miracles, still lacked faith in Him on most occasions (e.g., Matthew 16:7-9; 17:20).

While that was the norm, every once in a while, Jesus encountered someone WITH faith that genuinely amazed Him. One such example was the Roman centurion who had a sick servant. When Christ was told of the illness, He volunteered to go to the home of the centurion to heal the man. I must admit, if I was the centurion, I would have likely insisted Jesus make the trip. I'd want to watch it all happen. I'd want to ensure nothing got in the way. I'd presume Christ would have to touch the sick man for the healing to occur.

But that's not what the centurion did – far from it actually. As a soldier with authority over others, this man understood something that few others apparently did. Namely, that as God, Christ only had to give the command for the servant to be healed. Believing that, the centurion told Jesus to simply say the word and that would be enough. *When Jesus heard this, He was amazed and said to those following Him, "'Truly I tell you, I have not found anyone in Israel with such great faith'"* (Matthew 8:10).

If God has said it, we can trust it. Our faith can amaze God – let it be by its presence and not by its absence.

DAY 83 – FULFILLING

As Paul concluded the book of Colossians, he added a command to a guy named Archippus. We know very little about the man and even less about his ministry…which is wonderful, because it allows us to apply the command to almost **any** person with **any** ministry (which, by the way, should include all of us).

Paul's command to this mystery man was simply this – "*fulfill the ministry that you have received in the Lord*" (Colossian 4:17). *Fulfill* was derived from a word that meant *to see*, and conveyed the idea of *seeing to* something. It meant being aware of needs and seeing that they got met.

Because the requirements of any ministry can be burdensome, it's vital for us to understand that ministry is received "in the Lord." It comes from the highest authority, and therefore, it needs to be accepted and acted upon. But it also means that the work we've been given flows from the relationship we have with God. We need to remember that our ministry is IN the Lord because if we forget Whom we serve, we won't stay at it very long.

Lastly, I want us to see the way in which we're to accept our God-given assignments. In this context, *receive* literally meant to *aggressively take hold of* something, to readily claim it as your own. When we willingly take personal ownership of something, we happily look after it like nobody else.

Friends, receiving and "seeing to" a personal ministry is a key part of our earthly existence. Without it, this life just won't be as fulfilling as God intended. For we were created first and foremost FOR God. To worship Him, glorify Him, and serve Him.

Have you received a personal ministry from God? If so, are you *seeing to it*?

DAY 84 – PEOPLE, GET READY!

Now then, you and all these people, get ready…

It's a very simple sentence. Not long, not hard to understand. It's the context and the participants in the conversation that make these words unique.

As the book of Joshua begins, Moses has just died. The nation of Israel is in an awkward and vulnerable time. The only leader they knew during the exodus was now dead. Undoubtedly, many in the camp wonder what will become of them now.

Therein lies the beauty of the opening sentence. It occurs within the larger context below:

> *After the death of Moses the servant of the LORD, the LORD said to Joshua son of Nun, Moses' aide: "Moses my servant is dead. Now then, you and all these people, get ready to cross the Jordan River into the land I am about to give to them—to the Israelites. I will give you every place where you set your foot, as I promised Moses."* (Joshua 1:1-3)

What's the point? Simply this – **when a man of God dies, nothing of God dies along with him**. God's plans are not thwarted simply because one godly person exits the scene. God's message to Joshua, Moses's replacement, was this – "Get yourself ready, because I'm going to continue what I started! In fact, I'm going to complete what I started."

If the idea to enter Canaan had been Moses's plan alone, then it would have died along with him. However, when a plan we're involved with is God's will, then nothing will be able to stand against it. God will bring about what He's started – even if one of His chosen servants is removed from the equation.

Have you allowed yourself to become discouraged because a godly leader has passed off the scene? How can the story of Moses and Joshua encourage you to carry on?

DAY 85 – FIRM AND SECURE

Those sounding an alarm are everywhere. The gist of their warning is that if mankind does not drastically change this or that, we will destroy the earth in ten to twelve years.

Please understand that I'm a huge fan of Planet Earth – it's been a wonderful place to live – and I support commonsense efforts to care for the home God has given us. We're to be good stewards of everything – including Earth. Beyond that, however, I don't give in to the fear-inspired rhetoric.

In fact, if we believe in a sovereign God and the infallibility of Scripture, the children of God can rest secure in the future of His world. Listen to God's promise about our home:

> *The Lord reigns, he is robed in majesty; the Lord is robed in majesty and armed with strength; indeed, the world is established, firm and secure.* (Psalm 93:1)

Who reigns – man or the Lord? Since it is God, then only His plans for Earth will come to be. It is Christ, and not man, who is robed in majesty. It is Christ who is armed with strength. As a result, the world is established – it is firm and secure. He is the only one who could set it up; therefore, He is the only one who can take it down.

Friends, our planet has been firmly and securely established by God Himself, and it will remain until the day HE decides it comes to an end. But go ahead and recycle that aluminum can anyway!

My daily quiet time has brought me to the haunting book of Job. As I was discussing the book with one of my daughters, we concluded that in many ways, its overarching theme is mankind's desire to boil life down to one simple rule: Good things happen to "good people," and bad things only happen to "bad people."

Everything within us recoils when we encounter a story like Job's. Here was a man whom God, Himself, called "blameless, upright, God-fearing, and shunning evil" (Job 1:8), and yet he lost nearly everything within a matter of moments. In the pages that ensue, we read his account from the perspectives of God, Satan, Job, and Job's friends. We observe as fallen, finite mankind deals with intense personal suffering.

With the exception of the ending, there is tragedy at nearly every turn. We watch as he receives word that his ten children have died suddenly and that all his crops, livestock, and servants have also perished. Then, on top of those gaping wounds, here come his well-intentioned friends with their huge salt shakers, ready to rub a little in.

Today, I just want to look at Job's initial reaction to the losses listed above. Upon receiving the final crushing blow that his beloved children were dead, "*Job got up and tore his robe and shaved his head. Then he fell to the ground <u>in worship</u> and said, 'Naked I came from my mother's womb, and naked I will depart. The Lord gave and the Lord has taken away, may the name of the Lord be praised*" (Job 1:20-21).

What an amazing attitude the man displayed. He realized God had given him everything and could rightfully take it back at any time. As such, even in times of loss, Job could worship and say, "May the name of the Lord be praised."

What is your attitude toward the things you call yours?

DAY 87 – MY LAMP

You are my lamp, O Lord, and my God lightens my darkness (2 Samuel 22:29).

As David neared the end of his life, he concluded that God had always provided light by which he could walk. As the verse says, God doesn't simply provide a lamp, God IS the lamp. And if God is the lamp, His Word is the wick (verse 31)!

We're no longer very familiar with using lamps, so some reminders about lamplight may help. First, you must carry a lamp with you – it does little good if left behind. In that regard, notice that David calls God, "my" God…He was David's <u>personal</u> lamp.

Next, a lamp only illuminates far enough for a person to take the next step…it's a light for our feet and path (Psalm 119:105) – not the high beams in the car lighting up the road far ahead. And that's okay, for as one wise sage once wrote, "Life by the yard is hard, but life by the inch is a cinch." Yet the higher a lamp is raised the greater distance the light penetrates the darkness. How highly do you exalt God and His Word in your life? Remember, the higher you lift Him up, the brighter your path becomes.

Lastly, notice it's not THE darkness that God shines into – it's David's **personal** darkness. AW Tozer once wrote, "*We need never shout across the spaces to an absent God. He is nearer than our own soul, closer than our most secret thoughts.*" *Darkness* in verse 29 means *obscurity*. Ours is a personal God, serving as a personal lamp, lighting the way through personal and difficult issues – things in your unique life that stump you.

God longs to light YOUR path and He uses His Word to do so – hold it high.

It's all over the news and social media. I'm guilty of it, too, I'm afraid. It's a natural reaction that can happen before we even realize it. Though David wrote of it thousands of years ago, it's still relevant today.

> *Do not fret because of evildoers, be not envious toward wrongdoers.* (Psalm 37:1, NASB)

If we're honest, we'll admit that we do a lot of "fretting" in response to what we view as evil. Perhaps, like me, you think that the command is simply not to worry in such instances, and certainly that's part of what David intends. However, the word David used for *fret, charah,* means *to burn or be kindled with anger.* (It even looks like charcoal to me!)

When we view it this way, we may have to admit that we fret over a lot of things. Far too often, we get angry, and in that anger, we are capable of almost anything.

Thankfully, when Scripture commands us to avoid one thing, God generally provides something better as a substitute. In this case, we don't have to look far. In the remainder of the Psalm, we're told to: trust in the Lord and do good (v.3), delight ourselves in God (v.4), commit our way to Him (v.5), rest in Him and wait patiently (v.7), resist anger and wrath (v.8), and remain humble (v.11).

One last thought. David reminds us as he closes the Psalm that when we let an evildoer off our hook, that person remains on God's hook. We can rest easy because, *"The Lord laughs at him, for He sees his day is coming* (v.13).

Have a situation which has caused you to fret? Take a quick look at your options, and ask yourself, "Which is better – anger and wrath, or peace and rest?" The choice is ours.

DAY 89 – CONTENTMENT

247,352. So read the odometer on my wife's 2004 van. I know the day will come when ol' Lula Bell will have to be replaced. But as I sat behind the wheel of "her" car, I was thankful that Toyota built such a reliable vehicle. I was also thankful that during the last fourteen years, my wife has remained content; she's never requested a new car.

Yet contentment is elusive. Everything within us seems to demand that we have something newer, better, bigger. The same marketers who pushed the 2004 Sienna on us as the greatest thing since sliced bread, somehow made us feel cheated only a few months later because we didn't own the 2005 model instead! How does one say "no" to the demands of our culture and the demands of our own desires?

Paul tells us that contentment has to be learned (Philippians 4:11-12). *Contentment* comes from the Greek, *autarkeia*, which is compounded from *autós, self* and *arkéō, to suffice, be sufficient.* Literally, the word means *self-sufficient,* but not in the way the world defines it. It does NOT mean that we have no need of anything or anybody else. Instead, the word describes the Spirit-filled Christian who already has within all they need through the indwelling Christ! And Paul says we need to learn this through experience; to come to the realization that you + Christ = enough.

Don't get me wrong; driving an old clunker doesn't make us holier, and it's not wrong to replace things when and if necessary. But discontentment often sets IN long before our stuff wears OUT. So whenever discontent raises its ugly head, we can say no to it by reminding ourselves that we already have everything we need in Christ.

What role does discontent play in your decisions? How might it help to remind yourself that, with Christ, you already possess everything you need?

> *But godliness with contentment is great gain.* (1 Timothy 6:6)

DAY 90 – BROKEN PIECES

Their boldness was encouraging and humbling.

As God had ordained, the hotel I was staying at was a few blocks from the workplace of a college classmate. After I had a very pleasant visit with my old friend, the ladies manning a display outside the same store stopped me to speak with them.

They were representing Teen Challenge – a faith-based ministry working to free young women from abuse and addiction. I listened as Cheryl and Keirra (not their real names) told me of their past lives of addiction, sexual immorality, and all types of physical and emotional abuse.

Despite their pasts, these women couldn't keep the smiles off their faces. Not because they found any joy in the dark portions of their pasts, but because they knew what the Lord had rescued them from. Their enthusiasm was so great it was as if they were going to burst if they didn't tell everyone what Christ had done for them.

A few people stopped and listened, but most walked past. Perhaps the passersby were put off by these ladies' broken teeth or multiple tattoos. That's a real shame, because those who stopped saw a wonderful display of a fervent love for Jesus. These women were radically transformed by the love of their Savior, and they wanted everyone to know!

I was challenged by their example. These women loved their Lord much because they knew just how much they needed Him. I wonder if my frequent apathy about sharing my faith might be related to a proud misperception that I'm "really not that bad" – therefore Christ really didn't have to do too much for me. As a result, I don't have much desire to tell others what Christ has done. What about you?

> *I tell you, her many sins have been forgiven–as her great love has shown. But whoever has been forgiven little loves little. (Luke 7:47)*

DAY 91 – I THIRST

On the wall of each of her Missionaries of Charity chapels, Mother Teresa inscribed these words uttered by Christ on the cross – "*I thirst*" (John 19:28).

In her mind, Jesus' words expressed not only the human need of a dying man, but also the heart of the Divine. As Mother Teresa wrote, "We carry in our body and soul the love of an infinite, thirsty God. God thirsts. God thirsts for us and humanity thirsts for God." Yet God thirsts not from need, but from desire for us.

As we consider His longing for us, may our response to Him be a thirst of our own, similar to that expressed by the psalmist - "*As a deer longs for streams of water, so I long for You, God. I thirst for God, the living God*" (Psalm 42:1-2).

If you find yourself questioning the love God has for you, remember it was God's thirst for the lost souls of humanity that sent Christ to the cross. Just as He thirsted for you then, He continues to long for a close relationship with you now.

If you've ever flown on a commercial airliner, you know the routine. As part of the safety presentation, you've likely heard something along the lines of, "This aircraft is equipped with six emergency exits: two in the front, two over the wings, and two in the rear of the plane. Please take a moment to locate the exit nearest you, remembering it may be behind you." If you can't find an exit, you're frankly not looking very hard – because they're never very far away!

Those were my thoughts as I read the following:

> *No temptation has overtaken you that is not common to man. God is faithful, and He will not let you be tempted beyond your ability, but with the temptation He will also provide the way of escape, that you may be able to endure it.* (1 Corinthians 10:13)

I love the many reassurances in this verse. First, I like the reminder that temptation comes to ALL of us, and it comes in many different forms. Yet no temptation is unique to you – they've all been experienced by others as well. Next, we see that even in the midst of temptation, God is faithful. His faithfulness is demonstrated by providing the ability to endure temptation (without succumbing) until His way of escape is revealed.

Like you, I've endured my share of temptation. Thankfully, I can attest to the truthfulness of the verse above. In EVERY situation, God has made a way out and has even lit the floor to guide me to the exit. Sadly, I've occasionally ignored the warnings and chosen to remain in a doomed "plane" longer than necessary – but in His faithfulness, He continued to point the way out.

If you're facing a tempting situation, immediately look for God's nearest exit. Remember, it may mean backing up and changing courses!

DAY 93 – BROKEN GLASS

The loving cup is shared,
The crystal goblet smashed.
Their brave, determined, joyful heels,
Dance in the broken glass.

These words, taken from a poem called *Wartime Wedding**, were a tribute to a fictional couple who were married during the height of World War II. While this particular couple was fictional, the reality they represented is not. Countless couples married during the uncertainty of that war, yet did their best to make the most of it.

While I won't compare everyday life to the rigors of war, in many ways all of us face a world where our floors are covered with broken glass. Our lives are littered with debris that has accumulated from broken dreams, broken promises, broken bodies, and broken hearts. None of us dance very long before the effects of brokenness enter.

But what do we do once the brokenness arrives? Do we find a way to move on despite it? Do we continue to put on our dancing shoes and listen for the beauty in music? Or do we just stop seeing the wonders around us? Stop hearing our song? Throw in the towel of surrender, thinking joy is only a distant memory?

Take heart, Christian. While God never promised us a life free from broken glass, He makes a great partner for the dance! Will you allow Him to lead you across the floor?

> *There is a time to weep and a time to laugh; a time to mourn and a time to dance…* (Ecclesiastes 3:4)

***From *Rose Under Fire* by Elizabeth Wein**

DAY 94 – KEEP AT IT!

God asked the first question, and Isaiah asked the second. In the section my Bible calls "Isaiah's Commissioning," God asked, *"Whom shall I send? And who will go for us?"* to which Isaiah gave the iconic reply, *"Here am I. Send me!"* (Isaiah 6:8).

Yes, I love Isaiah's response, but today I want to focus on something else. After the question and answer above, God went on to describe Isaiah's task – to tell Israel to return to the Lord (verse 9). It was at this point that Isaiah asked *his* question about his new assignment.

> *For how long, Lord*? (verse 11a)

Isaiah wasn't concerned about where he should start, or how the people might react to his unpopular message; he only wanted to know if this was a "one and done" event. Was he to speak up once and then go home? What exactly was God's plan?

Here is the vital response from God:

> *Until the cities lie ruined and without inhabitant, until the houses are left deserted and the fields ruined and ravaged, until the LORD has sent everyone far away and the land is utterly forsaken.* (verses 11b-12)

In other words, "Warn them until there is nobody left to warn. Minister to them as long as there is anyone left to minister to. As long as there is any hope at all, you keep at it, Isaiah."

Friends, serving others in God's name can be wearisome. Witnessing to a world with largely unresponsive ears is discouraging. So, please let God's response to Isaiah encourage you today – as long as there is ANY hope of impacting the eternity of ANY person – keep at it!

DAY 95 – UNLESS IT'S DIFFERENT

Whether it is favorable or unfavorable, we will obey the Lord our God, to whom we are sending you, so that it will go well with us, for we will obey the Lord our God. (Jeremiah 42:6)

If ever there was a group willing to follow the Lord, it appeared to be the remnant in Israel. They had seen the judgment of God in response to the nation's idolatry, and they asked Jeremiah to give them instructions for obedience thereafter.

Knowing it may not be an easy message to hear, the people braced themselves for whatever God may say. They decided in advance that regardless of what they heard, they would obey. Whether it was favorable or unfavorable, pleasant or unpleasant, easy or hard, by golly, they were gonna do it! Or so they said…

Jeremiah took their request to God and waited for the Lord's answer. When it came, God's message was simply for the people to remain in Judah and live in peace. They were not to flee to Egypt in fear of Nebuchadnezzar (verses.9-12).

Stay put, don't run. What could be clearer? Yet, this was the remnant's response: *"You are lying! The Lord our God has not sent you to say, 'You must not go to Egypt to settle there.'"* (43:2). Sadly, Scripture tells us: *"So they entered Egypt in disobedience to the Lord"* (43:7).

Please don't miss this. The people knew in their heads that obeying God – no matter what it took – would be the better path. They knew it would "go well with them" to obey. But they had already determined in their hearts to flee. They had settled their course of action before hearing from God.

Yet we frequently do the same thing. "God, we'll do whatever you tell us, unless it's different than what we want to do!" Friends, God's Word is not a buffet table where we pick and choose the parts we like. We are meant to let His Word lead us, not pick at it. Choose today to obey all that's there.

DAY 96 – TEN WHOLE DAYS

Last time, we discussed the Israelites' stated desire to follow God's every command. Yet once they heard that command, they proceeded to do what they wanted anyway. Today, I want to look at one possible reason why.

You may remember that the people had approached Jeremiah, wanting him to go to God in order to receive a direct message from the Lord. A message they said they would follow (Jeremiah 42:6). But listen to how the very next verse is worded:

> **Ten days later** *the word of the Lord came to Jeremiah.* (verse 7; emphasis added)

I wasn't there, so I can't say for sure, but my suspicion is that when the people first asked for God's direction, they sincerely intended to follow Him. But an answer didn't come immediately, so they panicked and made their decision (to flee to Egypt) on their own. Fearing the Babylonians, they just didn't think their situation could wait. When God's plan FINALLY came, it was different than theirs, so they disregarded it.

Sound familiar? I can't tell you how many times I've done likewise. Some decisions we face (like Israel's decision to flee Canaan and go to Egypt) are major. We should take them to God seeking His guidance. But then, we need to wait. I know we live in a microwave culture. Our ability to wait is challenged in a twenty-four/seven, connected world. "Ten days, come on already, Lord! That's two whole work weeks! Chop, chop, God. We've got places to go and people to see!"

Friends, I know that sometimes circumstances force our hand and we must meet deadlines. But if we're honest, much of our hurry is self-imposed. When possible, let's take our requests to God and then wait to hear from Him – even if it takes ten whole days!

DAY 97 – SHORTCUTS

I was a little more than half-way through my Biblical Greek class. It had been a lot of fun and a LOT of work. Along the way I figured out that I really wanted to KNOW Greek, but I wasn't quite as interested in having to LEARN it. If only there was some magic way to acquire knowledge of the language without having to put in all the effort!

I thought the same thing as I was cleaning up the kitchen after dinner – if only I could have a clean kitchen and clean dishes, without having to spend any time and energy to ensure it! As I was emptying the dishwasher, I had to admit that in many ways I'm just downright lazy – especially about the things that I don't want to do.

Unfortunately, I know that I can be pretty lazy when it comes to my spiritual walk too. I want to be holy, but often I'm not willing to take all the necessary steps to be so. I want to know my Bible better, but I sometimes fail to pick it up. I want to more regularly hear God's voice, but I frequently refuse to slow down long enough to pray and listen to Him. In short, I want the results, but often refuse to spend the necessary time in His "gym."

For example, as Paul reminds us in Romans 5, there are no shortcuts in bringing about God's desired outcome. There we're told that suffering produces perseverance; perseverance, character; and character, hope. But, oh, how we'd love to jump immediately to the hope without having to persevere through anything or develop character. Yet generally nothing worthwhile is easy.

So persevere, my friends, and if we'll keep our eyes on the prize, we'll be too busy to look for shortcuts.

DAY 98 – IT'S NO SECRET

Jesus left that place and went to the vicinity of Tyre. He entered a house and did not want anyone to know it; yet He could not keep His presence secret. (Mark 7:24)

As Jesus walked the earth, the news of His wonderful works, His miracles, and His heart for tax collectors and "sinners" brought Him much notoriety. So much so that the crowds often made it difficult for Him to move about or even eat in peace. So when He entered the city of Tyre, He hoped to slip in unnoticed, just to enjoy a moment of quiet. Yet as the text states, He could not keep His presence secret.

As I contemplated the end of the verse above, my immediate thought was that we shouldn't be able to keep His presence a secret in our lives either. While we may not be able to perform the works and miracles He did, we can tell of them. And nothing should keep us from reaching out with His love to those we encounter. Christ should be such an integral part of us that wherever we go, He goes. Whatever we say should be words He'd say. What we do should reflect what He would do.

In short, we should live and love in such a way that we can't keep His presence secret – people should see Him clearly when they look at you and me.

Perhaps you've encountered them along life's road – folks who seem to leave a wake of destruction everywhere they go. For whatever reason, their presence is almost always associated with strife.

While I don't pretend to understand all people, and there are certainly exceptions to almost every rule, Scripture speaks of such individuals in general terms. In Proverbs 13:10, we read this:

> *Through insolence comes nothing but strife,*
> *But wisdom is with those who receive counsel.*

Insolence isn't a word we use frequently, and some translations actually prefer *pride*. The Hebrew word literally means *arrogance or presumptuousness*. In practical terms, I believe this verse states that when we presume that we already know everything, it reveals our sense of pride or arrogance. The result? Strife and contention – with everyone, over everything.

Thankfully, that coin has a flip-side, and the remedy for continuous strife is to receive counsel. If we want to get along well with others, Scripture instructs us to listen to one another. We need to take into account the thoughts, feelings, and opinions of others. To do so is not only kind and considerate – it's wise!

While not specifically stated here, the implication of the second half of the sentence is that receiving counsel takes grace and exhibits humility, and the outcome is likely to be peace and unity.

Take an honest inventory of your relationships. Are they marked mostly by peace and unity or by constant strife? Could it be that you're presuming that you already know all there is to know and don't require input from others? Any changes you need to make?

DAY 100 – BLESSED FOR BLESSING

The headlines screamed the need. People all around the country are at odds. Riots in the Northwest, protests in the Southwest, and anger throughout the rest of the land. Top political leaders actively encouraging the fanning of flames. A volatile word here, a cheap shot there. When will it stop?

If nowhere else, it needs to stop when it reaches you and me! Recently, I was reminded of (and challenged by) these words from Peter:

> *Do not repay evil with evil or insult with insult. On the contrary, repay evil with blessing… (1 Peter 3:9)*

I readily admit that when someone insults us, the knee-jerk reaction is to pick up some mud and sling it right back. Don't like what somebody did to you? Get even. Don't like what they said about you (or your favorite politician)? Drag them (or their people) through the mud too. It's understandable; shoot, it's easy. Easy, but not good. Easy, but not right.

Instead of doing the natural, understandable, easy thing, Peter says we're to repay the evil done to us with *blessing* – a word which here means *to speak well of others*. Why? The rest of the verse tells us:

> *…because to this you were called so that you may inherit a blessing.*

When we donned the "team jersey" as Christians, we accepted the call to act as Christ would – which includes loving our enemies. While behaving in a Christ-like manner today is a reward in and of itself, this passage also teaches that we'll one day inherit an eternal blessing as well.

Getting caught up in all the negative bickering these days? Instead of an insult, try returning a verbal blessing in its place. It may bring peace today, and it will definitely bring a blessing later.

DAY 101 – GOD WAILED

As a follower of Christ, you've likely encountered the occasional protestor who states they can or will not believe in a God who creates "people destined for eternal punishment" (or some similar wording). It's the contention that if there is a God, and if He creates people solely for the purpose of being eternally damned, they want no part.

Honestly, if God created man with a sadistic desire to watch them burn in hell, I would agree with them. IF that were God's intentions for man. Yet the consistent message of the Bible is that God takes no delight in the death and subsequent judgment of unrepentant men. Of His chosen people Israel, God stated, *"As surely as I live, declares the Sovereign Lord, I take no pleasure in the death of the wicked, but rather that they turn from their ways and live"* (Ezekiel 33:11).

But what about Gentiles? Does He have the same desire for them? While telling Jeremiah about the devastating future awaiting Moab (one of Israel's foremost enemies), God said, "…*My heart moans for Moab like a flute*…" (Jeremiah 48:36). Other translations say God wailed or lamented for Moab. The original word meant *to roar*, and it was used figuratively to describe deeply felt compassion or sympathy.

Friends, THAT is the heart of our God. It is His desire that none be lost, but all come to a saving faith in His Son (2 Peter 3:9). He created us not to damn us to an eternal hell, but to give us the opportunity to choose life with Him eternally. The truth is God does not send people to hell; they send themselves. The choice has always been man's; it continues to be today. His hand is extended to all; the door is open!

DAY 102 – THE GOLDEN ARM

I was encouraged to find some good news in the headlines recently. A report out of Australia indicated that one man, one solitary guy, had single-handedly saved an estimated two million babies with a unique gift that he has to offer. But the road he traveled to acquire that gift was costly to him.

At the age of fourteen, when most teenage boys are playing ball or hanging out at the local swimming pool, James Harrison was having an operation to remove a lung. It was during that operation that doctors believe Harrison developed a rare antibody in his blood. It is the antibody that allows pregnant women with Rh-negative blood to continue their pregnancies if the baby is Rh-positive. Without the antibody that Harrison possesses, the result is Rhesus disease, a condition that frequently results in mothers miscarrying or babies born with brain damage.

Hearing that he could help others, Harrison began donating blood as soon as he was allowed, and has made weekly donations for the last sixty years! The Red Cross in Australia has referred to him as "irreplaceable." Locals refer to him as "The Man with the Golden Arm," because, in Australia, nearly one in every five pregnancies involves Rh-negative moms, and for years, James Harrison has been the sole donor of the vital antibodies. Other people likely possess the antibodies, but they either are unaware they do, or they're unwilling to donate.

Folks, we all have a gift from God we can share with others. Please never underestimate the impact that a single life – yours – can have. And remember…that hardship you've endured (or are going through right now) might be the very thing God will turn into a unique gift that only you can give to others.

> *"And who knows but that you have come to your royal position for such a time as this?"* (Esther 4:14)

It was the story of Israel then, and it's the story of each person now. For a season, the Hebrews walked closely with God and followed His ways. Then, as in most relationships, one party began to drift away. As a just God, Yahweh was jealous as His children worshipped other gods. When they cried out for help, the Lord initially responded, "*Go and cry out to the gods you have chosen. Let them save you when you are in trouble*" (Joshua 10:14).

Finally, those who were guilty 'fessed up': "*Lord, we have sinned. Do with us whatever you think best, but please rescue us now*" (verse 15). In response to this plea, God sent a leader to deliver the Jews from their enemies. I just love that God showed Himself faithful – despite the repeated unfaithfulness of His people. But I was particularly moved by a statement Joshua included that described why God acted on behalf of His children:

He could bear Israel's misery no longer. (10:16)

Friends, that's our God. His love for us is so great that he cannot bear to see us suffer – despite the fact like Israel, we OFTEN deserve to. Because He cannot bear our misery in that sense, He sent Christ to bear our misery so we won't have to. But we must acknowledge our sin and believe He died for it.

If you've not done so already, call upon Christ who longs to redeem you from the misery of your sin.

DAY 104 – SAFE AND SECURE

I rarely remember my dreams. But, recently I had one that woke me up: I'd decided to walk home after enjoying the day at the beach. (I live in Missouri – hey, it's a dream!) But when I walked in the door, I encountered a group of robbers. They had pulled their van up to my house, removed all the doors (strange detail), and were in the middle of hauling out my washer and dryer. Upon hearing me, they fled.

I don't remember much beyond that other than feeling shaken and fearful. Unfortunately, "shaken and fearful" are the way many of us go through life. We spend billions of dollars annually on home security systems, handguns, motion detectors, security cameras, mace, and tasers. Our cars have alarms, and their remotes contain "panic buttons." We even track our family members by their cell phones. Why? Because we long to be safe.

I'm not immune to it, and I'm glad to have many of the items mentioned above. But despite them, I still apparently have subconscious fears and a need for security. What a relief it was, therefore, to wake up from that dream and read this during my morning quiet time:

> *"Because the poor are plundered, because the needy groan, I will now arise," says the Lord; "I will place him in the safety for which he longs."* (Psalm 12:5)

We're not told how God does this, but this verse tells us that He recognizes when others threaten us. He knows our need. And according to a plan we may not understand, God ushers us into the safety we all crave. That placement may mean protection here and now, or it may refer to the eternal safety of heaven. Either way, we can trust that God sees and takes action.

So, place your trust in Him and sleep well. Sweet dreams!

DAY 105 – THIS TIME. THIS GENERATION

For such a time as this. (Esther 4:14)

Most of us will recognize this phrase from Mordecai's words to his cousin, Queen Esther, asking her to approach King Xerxes in order to save the Jews. When I read the account recently, I was reminded of a similar life summary about David:

> *Now when David had served God's purpose in his own generation, he fell asleep; he was buried with his ancestors and his body decayed.* (Acts 13:36)

Although they lived nearly 500 years and 900 miles apart, David and Esther had this in common – God had raised them up to fulfill HIS purposes during THEIR generation. Yes, they were amazing and unique individuals whom God had set apart for incredible purposes. Yet you are an amazing and unique individual as well. And there is little doubt that God still wishes to use individuals in THEIR generation to accomplish HIS purposes.

Friends, why can't the people whom God uses today be you and me? In fact, if it's not you and me – who will it be? This is your generation. This is your time – what will you do with it? What is God calling you to do for Him?

DAY 106 – WHERE'S THE STRENGTH?

When David and his men reached Ziklag, they found it destroyed by fire and their wives and sons and daughters taken captive. So David and his men wept aloud until they had no strength left to weep. David's two wives had been captured—Ahinoam of Jezreel and Abigail, the widow of Nabal of Carmel. David was greatly distressed because the men were talking of stoning him; each one was bitter in spirit because of his sons and daughters. (1 Samuel 30:3-6a)

It's hard to imagine a more defeating scene. David returned to his hometown only to find it burned to the ground. Not only was his home destroyed, but his wives had been carried away. To top matters off, David's own men were threatening to stone HIM for what had happened.

What's a person to do when their world suddenly falls to pieces the way David's had? What would you have done? Where would you turn if those closest to you had turned against you? I purposefully paused in the middle of verse 6 to allow us time to consider these questions. Now let's look at David's response:

But David found strength in the Lord his God. (verse 6b)

The wording simply meant that David *grew firm or strong* in God. That may sound a bit vague and mysterious, but Scripture removes some of that mystery by telling us that David immediately went to God and asked Him, *"What shall I do? Shall I pursue this raiding party?"* (verse 8).

Friends, life throws us some wicked curveballs sometimes. Everything we once counted on may be pulled from under our feet. If you face such a situation, follow David's example and grow strong in God by seeking His direction. There really is no better option!

DAY 107 – NO GROUNDS

The book of Daniel is truly fascinating. Yet the details of its prophecies are so specific that it's easy to overlook some of the more practical parts of the story that can be applied to our lives today.

For instance, through his hard work and integrity, Daniel was appointed as one of the top 120 leaders in the kingdom. Even among those leading men, Daniel "*so distinguished himself…by his exceptional qualities that the king planned to set him over the whole kingdom*" (Daniel 6:3).

Out of pure jealousy, the other 119 leaders went on a witch hunt, trying to find anything in the way Daniel conducted himself which they could use to bring charges against him. After their massive investigation, here was their final report: "*They could find no corruption in him, because he was trustworthy and neither corrupt nor negligent. Finally these men said, 'We will never find any basis for charges against this man unless it has something to do with the law of his God*" (verses 4-5).

Folks, I'm far from where I want to be, but I'd love for everyone to be able to look deeply into my life and conclude that I was totally trustworthy, and free from all corruption and negligence. Oh, if the only fault people could find in me was my love and devotion for God.

How about you? Could what was said of Daniel be said of you as well? If not, what might need to change?

It was a "cut to the chase", "nuts and bolts" statement. Paul had been handed over by the Jews to stand trial in the Roman court system. He was initially held prisoner by the local governor, but knowing his rights, Paul appealed to Caesar.

Paul's appeal would eventually be granted, but before Paul was sent to Rome, King Agrippa sought an audience with him. The king basically asked Paul to defend himself against the charges brought against him.

I imagine that when one defends himself before a king, he chooses his words carefully, and attempts to express himself very clearly. When Paul had to succinctly define the message of grace for which he stood trial, these were his words:

> *I preached that they should repent and turn to God and prove their repentance by their deeds.* (Acts 26:20)

Repent literally means *to have a change of mind*, and as a result *choosing to walk in a different direction*. Accepting Christ, therefore, is making a conscious choice to stop walking away from God, and begin walking toward Him instead. But verbal agreement to the notion isn't enough. Paul said that if the repentance was sincere, if the entire course of one's life was truly changed, then there would be visible proof of that repentance. Jesus put it this way: "*You will know them by their fruit*" (Matthew 7:20). *Prove* in the verse above came from a word that meant *to weigh* and was used to describe how something *weighed in* on God's balance-scale of truth.

Friends, if your deeds were weighed on God's balance-scale, what would they prove about what you believe?

You can't live a perfect day without doing something for someone who will never be able to repay you. Coach John Wooden

What a great truth. Looking back, some of my best days were those spent lending a hand to others – including those I didn't know well or would never see again. There is a wonderful sense of accomplishment and pure joy found in giving to others and expecting nothing in return.

Right after teaching the Golden Rule (do to others as you'd have them do to you, Luke 6:31), Jesus defined what that looked like with His next words:

> *If you love those who love you, what credit is that to you? Even sinners love those who love them. And if you do good to those who are good to you, what credit is that to you? Even sinners do that.* (verses 32-33)

Loving others and doing good to them is always welcome. But loving and giving with absolutely no expectation of anything in return is even better. Wooden says it's the way to live a perfect day; Christ says it's the way to live the Golden Rule. And as a bonus, we'll one day receive a great reward (verse 35).

Looking to have a perfect day? Do something for someone who will never be able to repay you.

DAY 110 – A PROMISE BROKEN

It's a small point in a giant story. In fact, I overlooked it many times when reading the account between David and Goliath. After Goliath fell, we're told:

> *When the Philistines saw that their hero was dead, they turned and ran.* (1 Samuel 17:51)

Of course they did; what else could they do? Well, for one thing they could have honored the agreement that Goliath had made on their behalf. During the forty days leading up to the encounter with David, Goliath had taunted Israel's army and made this offer:

> *Choose a man and have him come down to me. If he is able to fight and kill me, we will become your subjects; but if I overcome him and kill him, you will become our subjects and serve us.* (verses 8-9)

This was supposed to be a man-on-man, one-on-one, winner-take-all proposition. However, when their man lost, the Philistines fled. Should it surprise us? No, not really. But it does serve as a good reminder that we shouldn't expect the sworn enemies of God to keep their promises to us! People without a fear of God have little incentive to keep their promises once those promises become inconvenient or costly to them. Lost people are going to behave like lost people – we should expect no different.

Sadly, the Philistines would have fared far better had they kept their promise. Once they decided to run, they gave up far more than their freedom – Scripture tells us their dead soldiers were strewn throughout the land. The second lesson this part of the story teaches is that keeping our promises is the better path to travel.

Are you surprised when people without Christ behave like they don't have Christ? Are you diligent to keep your word?

DAY 111 – COFFEE OR HOT WATER?

I knew immediately I'd done something wrong!

For years, my usual morning routine began by making a small pot of coffee in my Mr. Coffee Jr. Every day, I filled the decanter, poured the water into the coffee-maker, put the filter into place, added the usual amount of grounds, and pushed the "On" button.

However, one morning when I came back into the kitchen to pour that glorious first cup of coffee, something was definitely wrong. For there in the decanter was NOT rich, dark, savory coffee – just hot, slightly-discolored water! Sure enough, when I pulled out the filter, it was empty; I had somehow forgotten to add the coffee grounds!

While it was a silly oversight on my part, it provides an opportunity to apply a wonderful spiritual truth. When we put water through coffee grounds we expect to see coffee. If what we see instead is simply water, the coffee didn't "take." We have to pour the water back through the grounds until what we get is actually the coffee we desire.

In a similar manner, after a season of walking with the Lord, we should expect to see more of Christ and less of us. If after spending time in His Word, and attending His church we still don't bear any resemblance to Him, something isn't sticking! A child of God should take on an ever-growing likeness to the Son of God. The more we pour ourselves into Him, the more of Him should pour out of us.

Give it some thought…when others look into the decanter of your life, what do they see? Mostly just you? Or do they see Christ?

> "…put on the new self, which is being renewed in
> knowledge in the image of its Creator." (Colossians 3:10)

DAY 112 – MERCIFUL EYES

Remember your mercy, O LORD, and your steadfast love, for they have been from of old. Remember not the sins of my youth or my transgressions; according to your steadfast love remember me, for the sake of your goodness, O LORD! (Psalm 25:6-7)

Oh, how I relate to these words of David. When he stopped and sincerely considered his own life, David knew what was there. He knew it was a mixed bag: some good deeds, but also a lot of sin and mistakes. That reality led David to beg God to remember His mercy and His steadfast love for David instead of David's sin.

Honestly, that's my only prayer before a Holy God as well. If God chose to look on me and remember only my sins, I could never stand before Him; I could never approach Him and expect anything but rejection and judgment. I'd forever walk around in my well-earned guilt and shame.

But thankfully, through the finished work of Christ, our God's demand for justice has been fulfilled, and we can approach Him without fear, and be greeted with His love, goodness, and mercy.

Today, pause for a moment and thank Him for His merciful eyes; then extend that mercy to someone else.

DAY 113 – THE "SOME"

It was a fascinating experience. For weeks, my pastor and I canvassed the neighborhoods surrounding our new church building, inviting our neighbors to visit us. The responses were about as varied as the people we met.

We rang well over 500 doorbells and personally invited that many households. Honestly, if we decided to look at the return on our investment only in terms of numbers, we might conclude the effort wasn't paying off. However, after we spent only a week or two spreading the word, a handful of people entered our doors to worship the Lord with us.

If it were up to me, everyone who was invited would come; I'd always choose a 100% response rate, but such is never the case with any outreach effort. While the response from those we spoke to was largely warm and cordial, we also had doors closed in our faces and our brochures handed back to us. During those moments of potential discouragement, I reminded myself of Paul's evangelistic efforts in Rome. Listen to how Luke described them:

> *He [Paul] witnessed to them from morning till evening, explaining about the kingdom of God, and from the Law of Moses and from the Prophets he tried to persuade them about Jesus. 24 Some were convinced by what he said, but others would not believe. (Acts 28:23-24)*

Even Paul, arguably the greatest evangelist of all time, didn't persuade everyone. As verse 24 clearly says, some were convinced and some wouldn't believe. My challenge is to decide which "some" I will allow to impact me – will I continue to reach out to all in hope that some will respond? Or will I reach out to none because some will not? How about you?

Make new friends, but keep the old. One is silver, the other gold.

I don't remember where I first heard these wise words, but I love them for several reasons. First, they remind us of the importance of friendships. Whether we like to admit it or not, God created us to navigate this world alongside others, not to travel alone.

Secondly, they tell us that maintaining friendships requires effort on our part. It is one thing to make a friend – that can happen in an instant. However, to keep a friend takes consistent care over a lifetime. Yet it's worth it in the end. Time invested in a friend is never wasted.

Lastly, this little rhyme encourages us to remain open to making new friendships over time. We're to keep the doors of our hearts and lives open to others as they enter our sphere of influence. Our circle of friends should always be expanding, and our lives marked by inclusion and not exclusion as we share the love of Christ at every opportunity.

For those of you thinking this sounds exhausting, let me share a Family Circus cartoon that my sister used to have hanging on her refrigerator. The mother in the family was surrounded by several kids playing at her feet while she talked to a neighbor. The neighbor looks down at the mom's bulging tummy (she's obviously expecting another any time), and asks, "How will you divide your love between all of them?" The mom's wise answer was: "You don't divide love – you multiple it!"

Open the door of your heart and strive to make new friends while keeping the old. Remain closely connected to God – and He will multiple your love for others!

A friend loves at all times…(Proverbs 17:17)

DAY 115 – FALL FORWARD

Even if you fall on your face, you're still moving forward.
-Victor Kiam

Perhaps like me, you smiled when you read these words. I smiled because I've literally fallen on my face many times. My most spectacular "face plant" was in January of 1981 – you know it was good if I still recall it almost forty years later!
In short, I was attempting to walk to school on crutches across frozen streets and parking lots. Backpacks were not "in" then, so I was carrying all my books under one arm to boot. Well, you guessed it – one crutch hit a patch of ice and SPLAT – face first into the snow! I'll be the first to admit that it hurt, and I was terribly embarrassed. But looking back, the fact that I was even out there attempting to cover ice and snow on crutches was an indication of a willingness to try.

There were many obstacles, and yes, in that moment I slipped and fell hard. But I picked myself up, brushed myself off, picked up my books, and somehow hobbled into the school building a few minutes later.

In many ways our walk with Christ is no different. We're loaded with burdens. We're broken. There are treacherous spots all around us. We trip. We fall. However, if we're sincerely striving after the image of Christ, then even if we fall, we make progress because we're falling forward toward Him. Don't let a minor slip or even a major fall stop you. Get back up and continue the pursuit!

I press on toward the goal to win the prize for which God has called me heavenward in Christ Jesus. (Philippians 3:14)

DAY 116 – WHY THE APPLE FALLS

Millions saw the apple fall, but Newton was the one who asked why.
-Bernard Baruch

For many, faith seems to come somewhat easily. Perhaps parents taught them the essentials of Christianity and they readily accepted them as truth. The apple falls to the ground and that's simply enough for them.
For others, that's not the case. "Because someone said so", or "because the Bible says so" isn't sufficient for them. There's an internal questioning, a desire to understand more before accepting.

Surprisingly, God seems to welcome both! Of course He's joyful over a child who accepts Him without questions. However, He also welcomes prodigal sons and women at the well. Frequently, Scripture tells us to discern what we hear (e.g., 1 John 4:1) and to be like the Bereans who examined what they heard from Paul against Scripture (Acts 17:11).

Dozens of times Scripture encourages us to "seek the Lord." One instance reveals a close connection between such seeking and understanding:

> *The Lord looks down from heaven on all mankind to see if there are any who understand, any who **seek** God.* (Psalm 14:2, emphasis added)

To *seek* means to *inquire, study, or investigate.* God is not afraid of nature or science – He created nature, so the study of it doesn't concern Him. At the end of the day, however, there will always be gaps in our understanding – gaps that require elements of faith to believe.

God knows the way He created us; He can handle our questions. Take yours to Him today.

DAY 117 – FIRE EXTINGUISHER

One of my favorite things as a kid was watching Saturday morning cartoons. Not a week of Bugs Bunny, Daffy Duck, and Wylie E. Coyote seemed to go by without the frequent appearance of Smokey the Bear reminding us, "Only you can prevent forest fires!"

Smokey's words returned to my mind recently as I read Proverbs 26:20: "Without wood a fire goes out; without a gossip a quarrel dies down." We all know that some fires are welcome for the good that they bring – warmth and light. However, we also know that many fires are simply destructive – they demolish almost everything in sight. Such fires include angry arguments and vicious gossip – and God's Word says they need to be extinguished.

Thankfully, we all hold within our grasps one of the most effective "fire extinguishers" known to man – our refusal to participate. Angry arguments will fade if one or both parties will hold their tongue and cease (at least momentarily) from stoking the fire. Gossip, too, will become a cold ash heap if enough people refuse to stir the embers and add more wood.

When the fire burns around us, we can either throw on an "accelerant" with our harsh words or spreading gossip – or we can extinguish it with our held tongue. The choice is ours.

Throughout Psalms, we see evidence that David was not afraid to examine his life. Sometimes, I think that takes more guts than standing before Goliath. No wonder we tend to shy away from opportunities to be alone and silent with God.

In Psalm 19, David was contemplating the holiness of God as expressed through His law, statutes, precepts, commandments, and rules. As David considered God's holiness, he became painfully aware of his own sinfulness. In response to that awareness, David uttered this prayer:

> *Forgive my **hidden faults**. Keep your servant also from **willful sins**; may they not rule over me. Then I will be blameless, innocent of great transgression. (Psalm 19:12-13, emphasis added)*

David's goal was to be blameless and innocent before God, and he realized his only hope for that was for God to grant him forgiveness. Note that David asked God for two specific things: for his hidden faults to be forgiven, and to be kept from willful sins.

David understood that he was guilty of "hidden faults" – sins he had committed either inadvertently or out of complete ignorance. As mere men, we violate the holiness of God routinely and may not even be aware. But occasionally, we also willingly, knowingly sin against Him. I'm certainly not proud of it, but there have been times when I said or did things when I was completely aware that I shouldn't.

Perhaps you have knowingly told a "little white lie," exaggerated deductions on a tax return, withheld help for a neighbor, or threw in a verbal "zinger" solely to wound someone.

Today, spend some time examining your ways. Then ask God to forgive you of your hidden faults and to keep you from willful sins.

DAY 119 – MOST EXCITED

"Whatever you get the most excited talking about is god to you."

I don't remember where I first heard it, but I remember recoiling from it when I did. You see, at the time, if you would have asked me about myself and what I liked to do, I would have listed any number of things before God ever came up. You would have heard about my work, my wife, my kids, maybe even my golf game before I got around to God.

Please don't misunderstand; all of those things are fine – some are actually very, very important. However, none of them are worthy of being the most important in our lives. That spot is reserved for God Himself. Once He is firmly established upon the throne of your life, then all the other roles we play will fall into their proper place.

You see, there really is a practical difference between Jesus being our Savior versus Jesus being our Lord. As Savior, Christ makes it possible to escape the fires of hell in eternity. But as Lord He is the Master of our today. *Lord* is derived from a Greek word (*kuros*) that means *authority* and describes a person exercising absolute ownership rights. Both are obviously important, but which is emphasized by God? One indication may be that in all of the New Testament, "Lord" is mentioned nearly thirty times **more** often than "Savior." I'll leave it to you to draw your own conclusion!

Jesus as Savior is an essential beginning. But please don't stop there; allow Him to be Lord as well. When He is, you'll naturally get excited about talking to others about Him. So, what are you most excited to talk about today?

> *God exalted Him (Jesus) to the highest place… and every tongue shall acknowledge that Jesus Christ is Lord…* (Philippians 2:9,11).

DAY 120 – ENOUGH

Never will I leave you; never will I forsake you. (Hebrews 13:5)

It has to be one of the most comforting promises in Scripture. The God of the universe is with us – today, tomorrow, and forever. What joy and confidence that should give us!

Only recently did I notice the context in which this promise appears. The surrounding verses help us to better frame and apply the text. So in what context did God promise to never leave us? Here it is:

> *Keep your lives free from the love of money and be content with what you have, because God has said… "Never will I leave you; never will I forsake you."* (verses 4-5)

Panning out from the single verse gives us a better perspective of the promise. It is in the setting of money and contentment that God says, in effect, "Don't love money, and don't worry about stuff. Love Me instead, and I will be enough for you."

Remembering that God is always with us allows us to begin asking questions such as, "What would I do if money weren't a significant issue? What might God like me to try if fear of failure wasn't a concern? Am I staying in one work setting simply because I fear God won't provide me with a different job? Do I purchase stuff I don't need to win the approval of men?"

My friends, God is with you; He will NEVER leave you. And HE is enough – so free yourself from the love of money. Seek to love Him more instead.

DAY 121 – ACCEPTANCE AND EXPECTATIONS

*My happiness grows in direct proportion to my acceptance,
and in inverse proportion to my expectations.*
-Michael J. Fox

As a child, I enjoyed Fox's portrayals of Alex P. Keaton (*Family Ties*) and Marty McFly (*Back to the Future*) – such fun characters and fun times for Fox. However, fun times didn't lead to the statement above. While still in his twenties, Fox was diagnosed with Parkinson's Disease – a condition he has battled for nearly thirty years.

I don't know what Fox's beliefs are, but I know there are elements of truth in his words above. What seems to trip so many Christians up today is the expectation that faith in Christ equates to no real struggles in life. If we hold to such thoughts we'll constantly be frustrated, because a pain-free existence is not what Jesus promised – contrary to what you may have heard or believed. Consider just this one example:

> *I have told you these things, so that in me you may have peace. In this world you will have trouble. But take heart! I have overcome the world.* (John 16:33)

Please take time to notice the actual promise here – it is not a LACK of trouble, but the CERTAINTY of trouble that Christ promised. Peter reminds us that Jesus suffered to serve as an example for how we should endure the suffering that will come in this lifetime (1 Peter 2:21).

Despite what Disney may have taught us, the only realistic expectation is for hardship, not ease. And acceptance of this truth is the only way to avoid constant friction and frustration. Another word for it may be *surrender*. As I frequently tell my college students, when trouble hits (and it will), begin by questioning your fantasy and not your reality!

Constantly feeling frustrated by life? Maybe today is a good time to examine your expectations.

DAY 122 – TO OR FROM?

One of my favorite authors is Philip Yancey. I don't agree with everything he writes, but then again, after the passage of time and the gaining of new insight, I don't always agree with everything I've written either!

However, recently I was reading something in his book, *Vanishing Grace*, which I had to agree with. Not only that, but I had to acknowledge that I might be part of the problem he described and not part of the solution. Yancey noted the findings of a George Barna survey which found that 84% of college students personally knew at least one person they considered a committed Christian. Yet only 15% thought the lifestyle of those Christians was significantly different than anyone else's.

In other words, people recognized Christians by their words, but not necessarily by their actions. Yancey then goes on to state, "Christians must live in a way that differs from the surrounding culture or our message will never get a hearing…if we do not live in a way that draws others to the faith rather than repels them, none of our words will matter."

As one who spends much of my time dealing in "Christian words," this really got my attention. It has served as a good reminder that if my actions don't back up my words, my words just won't matter. And what a waste all these hours at the laptop will have been if the words are negated by the actions.

How about you? Do those around you know of your faith by just your words? Or do your actions confirm your words? Is your life drawing others to the faith or repelling them from it?

> *Live such good lives among the pagans that, though they accuse you of doing wrong, they may see your good deeds and glorify God on the day he visits us.* (1 Pet 2:12)

DAY 123 – FOLLOW EVERY LEADER?

To be honest, I was VERY tempted to skip over it; and who could blame me? The seemingly endless genealogies recorded in the first few chapters of 1 Chronicles are tough to get through! But I'm glad I persisted, because there, among a list of leaders of the tribe of Manasseh I found a hidden gem.

Seven men were named as being excellent leaders and heads of their clans. Scripture actually describes them with these glowing words: "*They were brave warriors, famous men, and heads of their families*" (1 Chronicles 5:24). Brave warriors, famous leaders – sounding pretty good, so far.

Unfortunately, that's not the end of their resume, for the next verse tells the single most important characteristic of these men. "*But they were unfaithful to the God of their ancestors and prostituted themselves to the gods of the peoples of the land…*" (v.25). Unfortunately, this critical failure to truly lead caused Israel to fall to the king of Assyria and the tribe of Manasseh to be taken captive into exile.

All too often we place the emphasis on the wrong things. We value looks, success, and fame – in ourselves and in those we're willing to follow. What does Scripture say is truly important? Whether or not we are faithful to God. Are we moving toward Him or away from Him? Are we leading others closer to Christ or, if they were to follow us, would we lead them into some form of captivity?

Faithfulness to God – it's an important quality in ourselves and a vital quality of those we choose to follow.

DAY 124 – THE OFFER

The names of the characters may trip us up, but otherwise it's a very intriguing story!

Balak was the king of Moab – a country between where the children of Israel were and where they were headed. Balak had heard all that the God of Israel had done to other nations that tried to oppose them, so he asked Balaam (a prophet in the region) to call down curses upon Israel. Balak figured that a cursed Israel wouldn't be able to triumph over a blessed Moab. So anxious was Balak to have Balaam curse Israel that he was willing to pay handsomely for the job to be done.

When the servants of Moab came to present the king's offer to Balam, this was the prophet's response:

> *But Balaam answered them, "Even if Balak gave me all the silver and gold in his palace, I could not do anything great or small to go beyond the command of the LORD my God."* (Numbers 22:18)

Several times the king continued to entice Balaam with riches, honor, and privilege, but each time Balaam refused to utter anything different than what God commanded him to say.

It's relatively easy to read these words on a page and think this was easy for Balaam. But, deep down we know it was probably much more difficult than meets the eye. For how many times have you and I compromised what God would have had us say or do for our own benefit – whether financial gain or acceptance by the crowd?

It's tough, isn't it? We like to be liked. We want to have our material needs met. But are we willing to compromise God's standards to have those needs fulfilled? Give it some thought – if you were Balaam, how would you have responded to the offer?

DAY 125 – GREAT ACTIONS

Great thoughts speak only to the thoughtful mind, but great actions speak to all mankind.
-Theodore Roosevelt

I don't know the context of Roosevelt's words above, but I appreciate their truth. Many of us enjoy discussing the Christian faith in philosophical, academic, or intellectual ways. I have no problem with that, because ours is a reasoned faith. It stands up to great scrutiny, and can readily be defended. However, we rarely "argue" a soul into heaven with our logic.

The skeptic would far rather "see" a sermon than hear one. People are less interested in how our faith looks on paper than they are in seeing how it works out in the trenches. Our chapters and verses won't attract their attention, but our actions will.

When we feed the homeless, volunteer at the hospital, spend time in the nursing homes, or visit the prisons, people notice. When we adopt children from overseas or foster children from across town, the world takes note. People may argue about or misunderstand what our faith **says**, but they won't argue or misunderstand the good our faith **does**.

Would you say you're a Christian more in word or in deed? Why not be one who both professes the faith and projects the faith to those around you? Remember, your great thoughts may be misunderstood, but your great actions won't be!

> *In the same way, let your light shine before others, that they may see your good deeds and glorify your Father in heaven.* (Matthew 5:16)

DAY 126 – HOLD THE HEM

It lets us see we can hold to the hem of His garment and still move forward.
-Frank Pomeroy

Pomeroy knows that of which he speaks. He is the Pastor of First Baptist Church in Sutherland Springs, Texas – the church which lost twenty-six of its members in a mass shooting in November of 2017. Less than eight months later, the church had a choice to make – host their annual Vacation Bible School (VBS) for the community or allow the shooter to claim one more "victim."

They chose to move forward. But doing so was a painful journey, as many of the slain had been important leaders in past VBS's. Yet throughout the congregation, other members stepped up and filled each open spot – and the turnout? Nothing short of amazing. Every year prior, the church's attendance was between forty and fifty children – that year, it swelled to over one hundred!

Why? Because the broken congregation chose to hold to the hem of Jesus' robe and move forward the best they could. Folks, I suspect many of us can relate to the picture painted by those words. Life may have knocked us to the ground, and we fear that we may never be able to get back up or move forward. At those times, perhaps the most we can do is hold on to the hem of Jesus' robe and remain there – just breathing at His feet as we hold on.

As FBC of Sutherland Springs discovered, Jesus binds up the wounds of the brokenhearted and helps us move forward when life knocks us down. Cling to Him.

> *He heals the brokenhearted and binds up their wounds.*
> (Psalm 147:3)

DAY 127 – ALL FOR ONE

If one member suffers, all the members suffer with it;
if one member is honored, all the members rejoice with it.
(1 Corinthians 12:26)

My late sister, Bernadette, used to love to say, "A burden shared becomes half the burden, and a joy shared becomes twice the joy." The Three Musketeers put it this way: "All for one, and one for all!" Sounds nice, but if we're honest, it's pretty tough to do. We often leave our wounded on the battlefield to fend for themselves.

As Paul told the church in Corinth, Christians were to dwell in such unity that no member was to live completely disconnected from the others. No, when a brother or sister in Christ suffered, <u>every</u> other member of their church family was to feel a bit of their pain as well.

I don't know exactly how that burden-sharing plays out, because every situation is likely somewhat different. But I believe there should be some sort of loving care and attention given to the one suffering. Mere acknowledgement that they are going through a difficult time likely does little to no practical good.

Think of someone you know who is currently enduring a hard season – what can you practically do to enter into their suffering with them? As much as it's up to you, don't let anyone within your reach go through their difficulty alone.

DAY 128 - BURNING SHIPS

In February 1519, with 630 men and eleven ships, Hernán Cortés set out to conquer Mexico and the Aztec nation. When word reached him that some of his men wanted to flee to Cuba, Cortes did the unthinkable – he burned all the ships, effectively removing his only means of retreat.

This isn't a history lesson, but history can teach us if we're willing to learn. One of the lessons we can learn from Cortés is that there are situations that demand our resolve to "burn the ships" which might allow us to retreat.

While there might not be any new geographic territories to explore in the twenty-first century, we are being forced into new social territories almost daily – many of which are increasingly hostile to our faith. I'd like to say these are completely uncharted waters, but history tells us what becomes of societies that throw aside the ways of God. We know what happens to cultures that deliberately walk away from His commandments and guidelines. Without Him, nations don't fare well; freedoms don't endure.

But as His children, what are we to do? Will we compromise with a world going mad? Will we sit quietly as the gap widens between the laws of God and the laws of men? Will we sit comfortably on our ships and drift along with the tide? Or will we draw some lines in the sand and take a stand? Yes, Peter told us to be in submission to all authority (1 Peter 2:13), but he also said, "*We must obey God rather than men*" (Acts 5:29). It takes great discernment to distinguish which response is best in any given situation. But as Edmund Burke once stated, "The only thing necessary for the triumph of evil is for good men to do nothing."

What will you do with your "ship"? Burn it so you won't turn back from Christ? Or relax on deck and let the tide take you where it will? The choice is ours.

Nearly every window was cracked. The passenger side door rarely opened. And the gear shift had to be wiggled between Neutral and Reverse before it would start. Sometimes the car literally jumped backwards when it was started! But what made that 1957 Ford station wagon a real terror on the road was its tendency to "pull to the right." If you let go of the steering wheel, you were on the right shoulder in an instant!

A simple front end alignment would have fixed it, but Dad didn't want to invest in a twenty-five year-old vehicle. Understandable – but if the driver wasn't always vigilant, they would have quickly gone off the road!

As I read the verse below, I remembered that "leaning car."

Do not let my heart incline to any evil... (Psalm 141:4)

In the beginning of Psalm 141, King David was praying to God for help – first for help controlling his tongue, then for help controlling his heart. Specifically, David asked that God wouldn't allow his heart to be inclined (or pulled) in the direction of anything evil. David knew himself. He knew that the natural tendency within him was to stray from the road of righteousness. His heart "pulled to the side" easily.

To his credit, David understood the waywardness of his heart and his own inability to stay on course. And unlike some of us, instead of trying to hide that weakness, David confessed it to God and begged for His help. David continuously needed his heart to be realigned back toward good – and He asked the only One capable of the task.

Is your heart leaning (even a little bit) in the direction of something ungodly? Ask God to bring you back into alignment with Him – He is faithful even when we aren't.

DAY 130 – PROTECTED

...no one will covet your land when you go up three times each year to appear before the Lord your God. (Exodus 34:24)

The significance of this verse had always escaped me. It's in a section of Scripture describing ancient Jewish traditions I've never practiced. Yet it contains a very practical truth for us all.

Three times each year, Jewish men were required to journey to Jerusalem for holy festivals. The occasions were Passover, the Feast of Weeks (fifty days later), and the Feast of Tabernacles (aka Harvest). Regardless of where he lived, an observant Jew would leave his home, his livestock, and his family to travel to Jerusalem for the celebrations.

That doesn't sound significant until we remember such a journey may have taken several days for travel, plus the seven or eight days that some of the celebrations lasted. So it's possible that each trip took two or three weeks. That's a LONG time to leave your family, land, and livestock unguarded! There were thieves in those days, too!

And that's where the promise from God comes in. Somewhat hidden in Exodus 34:24 is this promise from God to anyone who would listen: *"If you'll leave your land in order to be obedient to Me, I'll make sure you still have land to go home to. Come to Me and I'll protect you."*

Friends, the same is true today. At times God may call us to leave our places of comfort in order to be obedient to Him. We may fear losing things that we've typically called "ours." But our God is One who still protects and provides for those who follow Him!

Have you feared loss if you follow Christ more fully? Are you holding on to "stuff" too tightly? Do you trust that God will provide for you and protect you if you're obedient to Him? How can you apply this verse today?

DAY 131 – EXITS AND ENTRY RAMPS

Every exit is an entry somewhere else.
-Tom Stoppard

What a wonderful perspective for us to hold on to when our hopes don't go according to plan! Recently, I've watched helplessly as something I had hoped for just died on the vine. I had hoped and prayed. I had made plans, sought counsel, and rolled up my sleeves. Yet despite it all, it became apparent that this baby just wasn't going to fly!

The journey was coming to an end, and I needed to exit that highway. It was hard to admit it had ended before it really ever started. I felt like a failure, like I had misheard from the Lord months and months earlier. I firmly believed I had gotten on this particular highway in obedience to Him. Now I was sure, however, that one more mile on this path would be sheer disobedience. So exiting was the only option.

It was in this time of discouragement and defeat that Stoppard's words crossed my desk – and they made me smile. For with God as the pilot, there really are no dead-ends – only redirections. An exit from one path simply means finding the next entry ramp He wants us to try. The last outing need not be an ending, but rather the beginning of something new and wonderful with Him.

Remember – every exit from one plan is an entry to somewhere else God wants to take you!

> *A man's heart plans his way, but the LORD determines his steps.* (Proverbs 16:9, HCSB)

DAY 132 – THE RIGHT CONNECTION

I had spent the week at camp with a group of twelve year-old boys from the inner city. Ordinarily, I don't have much trouble forming connections with people, including those of different ages or cultural backgrounds. However, after the first couple of days with this particular group, I still felt like I had failed to reach them in any meaningful way.

Like Paul, I longed to *"become all things to all people, so that by all means some may be saved"* (1 Corinthians 9:22). By Day Two of camp I was literally wishing that I could become "Mr. Roy" – a twenty year-old African-American man whom the children naturally gravitated toward. I truly thought that if only I could connect to the kids the way he did, then something really great could happen.

But I didn't connect very well with them…in fact, if I'm honest, I failed them in so many ways. I seemed so very far from what they needed…BUT…something really great happened anyway. Half of the young men in my cabin accepted Christ as their Savior that week, and I know beyond the shadow of any doubt that was completely the result of the Holy Spirit working in the hearts of those boys. Never before had I seen God so clearly show Himself strong in my weakness.

I went to camp thinking the kids needed to connect to me, or to someone more similar to themselves, like Mr. Roy. But I couldn't have been more wrong. The One they needed to connect with was God – and He made sure that happened!

You see, I don't have the power to save; nor does Mr. Roy. Only the gospel has the power to do so, and I saw it firsthand that week. The great news is that the gospel is at your disposal to share with others too – will you?

> *For I am not ashamed of the gospel, because it is the power of God that brings salvation to everyone who believes.* (Romans 1:16)

DAY 133 – THE SOUND OF JOY

After the wall of Jerusalem had been rebuilt under Nehemiah's leadership, Jews who had been exiled in Babylon began to return to the city. As they did, they celebrated by dedicating the new wall to God. Nehemiah tells us, *"The sound of rejoicing in Jerusalem could be heard far away"* (Nehemiah 12:43).

As I read the account, I pictured a night in the late 1980's when my brother and I attended a Promise Keepers' conference in Boulder, Colorado. For reasons I no longer remember, we had to leave just before the event ended. As we walked to our car we could see the glow of the stadium flooding the nighttime sky. But it was the sound of over 55,000 men singing praise to the God in heaven that I remember most.

The sound carried for blocks surrounding Folsom Field. I read an account a few days later of an elderly woman who was a patient in a nearby hospital. She had told the nursing staff that she wouldn't die until she had heard the angels singing. **That night**, a window in her room was cracked open and the sound of joyful worship coming from Folsom Field reached her ears. She reportedly told the staff that she had heard the angels, closed her eyes, and died peacefully.

Whether we're rejoicing with thousands of others in a crowded stadium or worshipping alone in the privacy of our homes, a life of genuine joy is a rare thing that captures the attention of others. Can others hear any joy in your life? If not, what might need to change?

DAY 134 – NOT SEEN ON TV

It would make the best infomercial of all time. The "product" provides everything people seek. Among its many benefits were: long life, riches, peace, honor, pleasantness, and blessings.

If there was anything that could truly provide all of those things, wouldn't you rush out to buy it? Of course you would; so would I!

According to Scripture, all of these wonderful qualities are wrapped up in <u>wisdom</u> (Proverbs 3:16-18). No wonder we're told to obtain wisdom at any cost, and that we gain more from it than gold, silver, or precious stones (verses 13-15).

Part of the reason followers of Christ may chase the wrong thing is that we don't truly comprehend what wisdom is. Volumes have been written on the subject, and I have no hope of condensing all of it here. But the word *wisdom* conveys the idea of *having an understanding based on the knowledge of God*. With it is the skill to apply a God-based perspective to all life situations.

Regardless of how we define it, wisdom begins with a reverent respect for God. It is an acknowledgement that God is, and His ways govern the universe. Because that's true, wisdom will not be found within the pages of secular textbooks or on the front page of *The Wall Street Journal*. Worldly knowledge may be found there, but not godly wisdom. Vance Havner was correct when he noted that "many college professors are searching for wisdom while the janitors that clean their offices may have discovered it years ago."

Take a quick inventory – where are you searching for the answers to life?

> *Blessed is the one who finds wisdom, and the one who gets understanding, for the gain from her is better than gain from silver and her profit better than gold. She is more precious than jewels, and nothing you desire can compare with her.* (Proverbs 3:13-15)

DAY 135 – NOT ASHAMED

It's another of what I've come to call "bookend" passages – where an idea is introduced in one verse and concluded a few verses later. And in between are the "guts" of the message!

The passage I have in mind is 2 Timothy 1:8-12. It begins with Paul telling Timothy not to be ashamed of the gospel (verse 8). It ends with Paul telling Timothy that he himself is not ashamed of the gospel – even though he is in prison and about to be executed for preaching it (verses 11-12). But stuck in between those verses are the reasons WHY Paul is not ashamed, why Timothy should not be ashamed, and why you and I need not be ashamed either.

> *He has saved us and called us to a holy life—not because of anything we have done but because of his own purpose and grace. This grace was given us in Christ Jesus before the beginning of time, but it has now been revealed through the appearing of our Savior, Christ Jesus, who has destroyed death and has brought life and immortality to light through the gospel.* (verses 9-10)

Why was Paul unashamed of the gospel? Let's take a look. 1). By the gospel, Paul was saved from his sin and called to a holy life. 2). The gospel overcomes death. 3) The gospel brings life and immortality!

Only the gospel – the message of God's grace manifested through Christ, destroys death, rendering it *inert, completely inoperative, or totally without force.* At the same time, the gospel brings life that is *immortal* – a word that means *lacking the very capacity to decay.* And as Paul reminds us in verse 9, this is not because of anything we have done, but because of God's purpose and amazing grace!

Have you backed away from sharing the gospel for any reason? If so, spend some time contemplating the reasons why Paul says we need not be ashamed.

DAY 136 – GOD'S INVESTMENT STRATEGY

Once a year, my investment advisor pulls me into his office to review my "investment strategy." It's a somewhat painful experience because he wants me to be more aggressive, and, well, I'm just not! It's a constant balancing act between risk and return – I want good return but am unwilling to take much risk. Sound familiar?

My chats with my advisor come to mind when I think about the investment strategy God laid out for His children. Surprisingly, it's considerably different than what I've heard from former churches and many friends. Most of my peers fall into one of two camps – either the tithe is a bare minimum for the Christian, or the tithe has no place for the Christian (i.e., that was an Old Testament command only).

But here is God's strategy for those living in the age of grace:

> *Remember this: Whoever sows sparingly will also reap sparingly, and whoever sows generously will also reap generously. Each of you should give what you have decided in your heart to give, not reluctantly or under compulsion, for God loves a cheerful giver. (2 Corinthians 9:6-7)*

What's God's strategy for us? Give cheerfully and generously! Why? Because He loves a cheerful giver, and He will give back to us generously (in whatever ways He chooses)! And for those of you who fear that giving to others may leave you shorthanded, look at God's promise:

> *Now he who supplies seed to the sower and bread for food will also supply and increase your store of seed and will enlarge the harvest of your righteousness. (verse 10)*

Friends, sow your seed generously and God promises two things – you will reap generously, and you'll never run out of seed. Low risk, high return – pretty good strategy if you ask me!

DAY 137 – UNDERSTANDING

At the urging of one of my daughters, I recently reread George Orwell's *1984*. At one point, the main character, Winston, made a statement that caught my attention. "Perhaps one did not want to be loved so much as to be understood."

While it's one sentence from fiction and not from Scripture, it does highlight a deep-seated human need – to be heard and understood. Taken to excess, it can turn into one insisting that others hear and accept their opinion only; but that's not what I'm referring to here. I have in mind a pure need to know that another person we're sharing our heart and mind with has genuinely listened and heard us.

There is little doubt we all long for understanding as we journey through this life. But, like it or not, we can't make others want to listen and understand us; however, we can offer it to others. I believe listening, with the intention of understanding another, would fall under the "Golden Rule" – to do to others as we'd have them do to us (Luke 6:31). It would also easily fit within Paul's instructions when he wrote, "Do nothing from selfish ambition or conceit, but in humility count others more significant than yourselves. Let each of you look not only to his own interests, but also to the interests of others" (Philippians 2:3-4). We can't humbly look to the interests and needs of others if we don't understand what they are!

As I first read Winston's words, I was immediately reminded of the Prayer of St. Francis. Oh, that our heart's desire would be reflected by his words below:

> *O Divine Master, Grant that I may not so much seek*
> *To be consoled, as to console;*
> *To be understood, as to understand;*
> *To be loved, as to love.*

In addition to loving others, let's add a genuine effort to understand them.

DAY 138 – THE GOOD OL' DAYS

I've occasionally been accused of being too sentimental –
especially for a relatively young guy. Yes, it's true; I do look back
on many things with great fondness. Is that a crime?

No, it's not criminal. However, if taken too far, it may not be wise
either. In fact, the wisest man who ever lived confirms that living
life looking over our shoulder is foolish. Specifically, Solomon said
this:

> *Do not say, "'Why were the old days better than these?"*
> *For it is not wise to ask such questions.* (Ecclesiastes 7:10)

Obviously, the problem is not in making memories and
occasionally remembering them fondly. The problem occurs when
we constantly compare life today with some romanticized version
of days gone by. To hold every modern situation up to the
glamorized "good ol' days" is, in essence, to compare the worst of
today's events to the best of yesterday's. In that light, today has
absolutely no hope of measuring up. The result? We live each
day with a vague sense of dissatisfaction, missing all the good
they may contain. Believe it or not, these are "the good ol' days"
that the next generation will look back on!

I understand that in some ways it may appear that the old days
were better than now. However, the answer is not to live in
yesterday while cursing the problems of today. Instead of looking
in the rearview mirror, perhaps we should begin each day asking
God how we can make today the best it can be, bringing Him the
most honor and glory.

Ever notice that the rearview mirror is tiny compared to the
windshield? There's a reason for that – we're to look forward
more than behind us. Remember, it's difficult to fully embrace
today if we're still holding on to yesterday.

DAY 139 – ALTERNATE FACTS AND FAITHS

It's not information overload; it's filter failure.
-Maria Zayats

By many estimates there are now over a BILLION websites on the
internet. Each day, another 144,000 sites take flight (or attempt
to)! By the time you finish reading this message, another 100 to
200 new sites will hit the web.

Staggering, isn't it? The amount of information available begs the
question of "who can I trust?" The advent of "alternate facts" only
elevates the need for us to know where we can get reliable
information. Perhaps it even raises doubt about whether or not
there is any real truth to be found.

As the amount of information continues to grow exponentially, our
ability to comprehend it all shrinks. Therefore, our need to filter
out all the "fluff" and distinguish it from the fundamental becomes
more important, especially in matters of faith. To accept that all
faiths are the same is to experience "filter failure." We must make
our way back to these stabilizing words of Christ:

> *I am the way and the truth and the life. No one comes to
> the Father except through Me. If you really know Me, you
> will know my Father as well.* (John 14:6-7)

Perhaps to some, these words seem archaic, but the truth
remains – you were created to know God and to be known by
Him. And the truth is, that relationship begins with Christ. The
Christian faith is the only one in which God takes the initiative,
reaching down to save mankind. Every other major religion is
based upon man's best efforts to climb to Him.

Two hundred new sites are out there since you began reading.
Many contain "alternate faiths." How will you sort through the
misguided or actively deceptive ones? Remind yourself today that
Jesus is the truth.

DAY 140 – CHANGES AND CHANCES

We all have big changes in our lives that are more or less a second chance.
-Harrison Ford

As a general rule, I dislike change! For example, my home office is arranged the way it is because I LIKE it that way! If I have my preference, it will never change! In the work world, I belong to the group of folks known as "late adapters" to change. That's just a nice way of saying we go kicking and screaming!

Obviously, outside of the very small things completely within our control (aka my home office), change is a huge part of life. If we're unable to adapt or adjust quickly, we'll end up pretty miserable. I guess that's why I appreciated Ford's perspective above. Changes don't have to be viewed only as an end to the way we had things and preferred them. Changes can become second chances.

A lost job can become a second chance to pursue a different field altogether. Retirement can become the second chance to travel or volunteer. An empty nest can become a second chance for a parent to go to school this time. The lack of wind in the sails can become a chance to try water skiing or fishing, and so forth.

While Jesus is the same yesterday, today, and forever, not much else is! As a result, change is going to come. Instead of fighting it, look for the opportunities that the change may create. Ask God how He can use your life changes as new chances to serve Him more.

Jesus Christ is the same yesterday and today and forever.
(Hebrews 13:8)

DAY 141 – START. USE. DO.

The poor. The homeless. The hungry. The unbelieving.

All around us are people with needs that are so overwhelming it can be difficult to know where to begin. And if we're honest, the size of the need is so intimidating it's tempting to not even try. If we can't end the problem, we may think, "Why begin?"

Perhaps you've never thought such things, but I sure have. That's why I appreciated the words below from tennis great Arthur Ashe:

> *Start where you are. Use what you have. Do what you can.*

His words are neither overly optimistic nor pessimistic – like Baby Bear's porridge, – they're "just right!" I find in them realistic encouragement. Where do we begin? Look around in your immediate surroundings. There is someone within your reach today who could use your help. You don't have to take out a loan or learn a new skill; God will use what He's already given you to benefit those within your current reach.

Lastly, go into it knowing that you won't single-handedly cure the bigger problems. You can't feed the world, but you can feed one person for one day! God only expects you to do what you can – but He does expect you to do that much!

John put it this way:

> *If anyone has material possessions and sees a brother or sister in need but has no pity on them, how can the love of God be in that person? Dear children, let us not love with words or speech but with actions and in truth.* (1 John 3:17-18)

Start with those you already see. Use what God has given you. Do what you can to show His love through your actions.

DAY 142 – OUR EYES

We do not know what to do, but our eyes are on you. (2
Chronicles 20:12)

Were these the words of a lowly, incapable individual? Was this a
feeble admission of weakness by someone who had no ability to
figure out a simple problem?

Hardly. This was the conclusion of Jehoshaphat, one of the best
kings of Judah. Yet at the moment he uttered these words to God,
his nation was facing an onslaught of attack from a huge coalition
of armies. He knew that he was outnumbered and that he had no
natural means by which to withstand his enemies.

Surrounded, under attack, overwhelmed, hopeless, helpless,
discouraged, confused, no options, no way out – been there? Can
you relate? God seems to allow at least one such experience in
most of our lives at some point. What should be our response
when we find ourselves up against such a wall?

I think Jehoshaphat gives us a pretty good example – take our
situation to God and admit our need. Then, we keep our focus on
Him as our source of provision and guidance.

Lord, we may not know what to do, but help us keep our eyes on
You.

DAY 143 – FOR THE SAKE OF…

Occasionally, I hear a joking, "Shut up, Dave!" from the back of the classroom when someone thinks the lesson's point strikes a little too close to home. It's never my intention to unnecessarily make anyone uncomfortable; Scripture's truths tend to do that on their own! And believe me, nobody's conscience gets poked more often than my own.

That's exactly what happened when I recently read these words from David's pen:

> *Since You are my rock and my fortress, <u>for the sake of Your name</u> lead and guide me. (Psalm 31:3,* emphasis added)

I have no problem with the beginning of the verse – I love to think of God as my rock and fortress. Such thoughts bring reassuring comfort in a world that's shifting and unstable. So that part's fine. I also have no problem with asking God to lead and guide me – heaven knows I need His direction. So far, so good!

It's that five-word prepositional phrase in the middle that makes me want to say, "Quiet down there; that's getting too close to home!" Why? Because I know that many – dare I admit, most – of my prayers are not uttered with the same purpose in mind. No, my prayers tend to have "for the sake of Dave's name" in mind much more than "for the sake of YOUR name."

David's prayer was for God to lead him in whatever ways would bring the most honor and glory to the Lord, not himself. David loved and trusted God enough to place the course of his life in God's hands. It sounds a bit like risky business until I remember that God is so much more capable than I am. So I'm going to consistently give it a try – join me?

Lord, for the sake of Your name, lead us.

Twenty years later, he would have to face him again.

As Jacob returned to the land of Canaan, word reached him that Esau was coming to meet him – with 400 of his men! Understandably, Jacob cried out to God, "Please deliver me from the hand of my brother, from the hand of Esau, for I fear him, that he may come and attack me…" (Genesis 32:11).

Jacob had every reason to be afraid. The last he had heard from his brother, Esau had threatened to kill him for stealing his birthright and his blessing. The arrival of the man, along with 400 soldiers, would cause anyone to quake in their boots. Jacob remembered his wrong; he remembered Esau's threat to get even (resulting in his current fear). But then Jacob remembered something else – the promise of God.

> *But you said, "I will surely do you good, and make your offspring as the sand of the sea, which cannot be numbered for multitude." (verse12)*

When faced with very real fears and very real dangers, Jacob fell upon the very real promises of God. And we can do the same today. God hasn't promised us offspring as numerous as the sand of the sea, or that we'll become a great nation, but He has promised to never leave us (Hebrews 13:5). And, regarding fear, Jesus once said:

> *Are not two sparrows sold for a penny? Yet not one of them will fall to the ground outside your Father's care. And even the very hairs of your head are all numbered. So don't be afraid; you are worth more than many sparrows.* (Matthew 10:29-31)

Are you fearful today? Fall upon God's promises.

DAY 145 – FAKE ART

In his book *Love Does,* Bob Goff tells the story of his first fine art
purchase. For months he admired the painting in the gallery's
window. Finally, he broke down and made the purchase.
On the day he picked up his new prized possession, he was
surprised when the seller brought out two paintings – the original,
along with a fake reproduction. When questioned, the seller told
Goff that he should display the fake model and store the original in
a safe location to protect it and preserve its value.

As Goff tells it, he did just the opposite – he threw the fake in the
closet and displayed the original prominently in his home where
he could enjoy it daily. Just as the seller had warned, a few
months after making the purchase, the original got damaged – but
Goff didn't care. In his thinking, the artist didn't create the
masterpiece to be locked away, safe from all possible harm. I
admire his grit.

The Master Artist (God) has created many wonderful
masterpieces (us) – yet we're tempted to hide the real thing away
while we display a cheap substitute. In our efforts to protect
ourselves from all harm, we rarely allow the "real us" to be seen
by others. How tragic. And how sad for the Artist to see His work
hidden away.

Friends, Scripture tells us that we are the pinnacle of God's
creation; we are His finest craftsmanship. He didn't create you to
be hidden safely away. Be real. Be honest. Take some
chances. Yes, you may get damaged along the way, but
remember – God delights in what He created. Don't put a fake
substitute on display.

> *For we are God's handiwork, created in Christ Jesus to do
> good works, which God prepared in advance for us to do.*
> (Ephesians 2:10)

DAY 146 – GO YOUR WAY

Out of curiosity, I searched "end-times prophesy books" on Amazon, and got over 6,000 results. It's strange to me that God withheld additional details about the end of days from the likes of Daniel, but supposedly gave them to others selling books!

While rereading the book of Daniel, I stumbled upon a small phrase which carries big meaning. In fact, it's the very last sentence in Daniel's book. After giving Daniel numerous visions and explanations about His plans for the world's conclusion, God said:

> *As for you, go your way till the end. You will rest, and then at the end of the days you will rise to receive your allotted inheritance.* (Daniel 12:13)

It was so important that God said something very similar in verse 9 of the same chapter. "Go your way, Daniel, because the words are rolled up and sealed until the time of the end." In a sense, God was letting Daniel know He had said everything on the topic He intended to, and Daniel should not worry about or search after further detail.

Instead, Daniel was to tuck what he knew about future events away in his mind and get on with life. Again, if that was God's message to a prophet of end-time events, do you think He would tell us something different today?

Friends, God created this world. He knows the days and times He has appointed for it. It will end when He determines. We should live in light of that truth, but we should not spend much time trying to pinpoint timelines and events He has chosen to keep hidden. Instead, I believe He'd say, "Go on your way; live your life."

DAY 147 – MY STAY

They confronted me in the day of my calamity, but the Lord was my stay. (Psalm 18:18)

To better understand the beauty of David's words above, it helps to realize when and where he wrote them. David was in extreme fear for his life as he fled from an insanely jealous and murderous King Saul. He felt surrounded and near the end, but David knew that God was his "stay."

In ancient days, *a stay* was a type of staff used for support as travelers on foot made their way along uneven terrain. It was something they could lean on for rest or support. In other verses, the same Hebrew word is translated as *supply*. Either rendering beautifully fits our verse above – for in David's hour of need, God was the One who David could rest in and lean upon. God was also David's sole provider.

In the verse that follows, we see the motivation behind God's rescue of David. Simply put, God chose to rescue David because He delighted in him. The Lord does the same thing today because God desires to be with His created ones.

On whom or what are you leaning in your hour of need? Determine today to make God your support and your supply; He delights to provide for you.

DAY 148 – STANDING BETWEEN

It's an obscure Old Testament scene that is rarely (if ever) preached, yet I found it fascinating. In it, some of the Israelites had grumbled to Moses about what they perceived as unfair treatment. They believed God had intended for more than just the Levites to serve as priests in the tabernacle.

Moses assured them that he had heard God correctly, and God backed Moses up by literally having the earth open up and swallow those who stood in opposition. Surprisingly, however, more of the Hebrews continued to argue against Moses and God. This time, God's wrath was set to come against the entire Hebrew camp in the form of a rapidly-spreading, deadly plague.

Upon seeing what was happening, Moses immediately sent his brother, Aaron, out among the people to make atonement for their sin by burning incense. Listen to how Scripture records what happened next:

> So he placed incense on the coals and made atonement for the people. He stood between the dead and the living, and the plague was stopped" (Numbers 16:47-48).

As I thought about the scene, I realized that we have a lot in common with Aaron. No, we're not fighting plagues with incense, but figuratively speaking, we do stand between a just God and sinful men who face certain spiritual death and an eternal judgment. Like Aaron, we hold the answer to their deadly plague in the form of God's message of love and redemption available through Christ.

In that sense, we stand between the spiritually dead and the spiritually living every day – but are we concerned enough about those who are dying to share the gospel with them?

DAY 149 – THE UP

> *If then you have been raised with Christ, seek the things that are above, where Christ is, seated at the right hand of God. Set your minds on things that are above, not on things that are on earth.* (Colossians 3:1-2)

At this point in his letter to the Colossians, Paul began addressing the practical aspects of following Christ. And his opening comment sets the stage. Specifically, we're told *to seek* and to *set our minds* – on things above.

The language Paul used for *seek* meant to *continuously search, getting to the bottom of a matter.* I actually like the NASB here because it emphasizes the ongoing nature of this pursuit by saying "keep seeking the things above."

The next thing we're instructed to do is to *set our minds* on things above. Interestingly, this phrase conveys the notion of *developing an inner perspective which shows itself in outward behavior.* We're to concentrate on things above with the intention of allowing what we find there to impact our actions.

But what are the "things above" we're to strive after? Upon what things are we to form our opinions and base our actions? Believe it or not, we're not specifically told. In fact, "things above" does NOT even appear in the Greek text which literally reads: "If then you were raised together in the Christ, the up seek, where the Christ is in right of the God sitting; the up think, not on the earth."

The Up, seek…The Up, think. Period. All we know is that it's not things on earth and it's where Christ now sits.

Amazingly, "up" here **can refer to either place or time**. In other words, we're to continuously strive for and think about our place in heaven which is above – and our time in heaven which is up above.

The things of this world got you down? Think Up!

DAY 150 – VIRTUALLY IMPOSSIBLE

"But <u>it</u> will never be a substitute for the face of a man, with his soul in it, encouraging another man to be brave and true. Never try it for that. It will break down like a straw."

If I were to ask you to guess, what do you think "it" is? Money? Power? Drugs? Sex?

Believe it or not, the above quote was taken from *The Wreck of the Golden Mary*, an 1856 work from Charles Dickens. And "it" was the invention of the telegraph. As Dickens's character astutely predicted, it's human nature to take an electronic invention and substitute it for real human interaction. Modern technology allows us to remain "connected" from a distance, so we remain distant. Because technology allows for easy connection in that way, less effort is often made to physically get together.

That's true for every family – including God's family. More and more frequently, God's children are avoiding gathering with God's family in God's house. Instead, it's tempting to catch a worship service on TV, via live streaming or podcast. Those are marvelous options for shut-ins, for or a rare exception. However, virtual church as the mainstay of Christian fellowship lacks some vital elements. It is virtually impossible to exercise the "One Another"s of Scripture (love one another, lift one another up, encourage one another, share one another's burdens, etc.), if we never spend actual time with one another. Pretty hard to help out in the nursery, too!

Have you gotten out of the habit of participating with a local church? Why not re-engage this week?

> *And let us consider how we may spur one another on toward love and good deeds, not giving up meeting together, as some are in the habit of doing, but encouraging one another—and all the more as you see the Day approaching.* (Hebrews 10:24-25)

DAY 151 – ONLY ME

I have been Yahweh your God ever since the land of Egypt; you know no God but Me, and no Savior exists besides Me. (Hosea 13:4; HCSB)

"No Savior exists besides Me." It's a bold statement that brings hope and comfort to millions, but offends others. Yet it's a claim which God alone can make, and one He alone can fulfill.

God made this statement in the context a warning He had given to Israel. The Hebrews had wandered from God's path and were at risk of being judged and punished. But included with the warning was an offer of a "way out," a means by which to be saved.

Other religions may offer great teachers, paths to personal peace, promises of prosperity, and so on. However, man's greatest need is not knowledge, peace, or material wealth. Ultimately, man's greatest need is to be redeemed from his sin. And at the end of the day, Christianity is the only religion in which God Himself paid the ransom to buy mankind back. Every other set of beliefs center on man's ability to please God through their efforts.

To those wayward Israelites, God beckoned through Hosea:

Take words of repentance with you and return to the Lord. (14:2)

Friends, God's instructions for salvation are the same today. Stop going your own way. Turn around. And return to the Lord. Those who do so will find joy instead of judgment.

DAY 152 – THE WIND

If I'm honest with you, many days I just don't "get it." I don't see what in the world God is up to – in my life or in the world around me.

I know that His Word says He is active in every detail. Not only that, but He is working together every single action, word, decision, accident, and circumstance in my life for good. Which good? – To transform me into the image of His Son. (Romans 8:28-29).

But, let's face it, transformation from who we've always been into who He wants us to be is often a very slow and painful process. Many days I groan at my own lack of progress; I'm frequently weary of facing the same battles day after day, wondering if I'll ever finally take that hill. Yet onward we march with each day, believing, even if not seeing, that our Heavenly Father is faithfully keeping His promise.

Even Solomon, the wisest of men, was baffled as he wrote these words: "*As you do not know the path of the wind, or how the body is formed in a mother's womb, so you cannot understand the work of God, the Maker of all things*" (Ecclesiastes 11:5).

Trying to figure out the Infinite One with our finite minds is like trying to trace the path of the invisible wind or knowing how an embryo develops into a newborn. We can't see either with the naked eye, but we know there's something occurring just the same.

Friends, even when you can't sense it, even when He seems distant and uninvolved – yes, even then, your Maker is actively knitting together the details of your life. Trust Him.

As I type, I'm preparing to make the cross-country journey to attend my uncle's funeral. Already, I anticipate the tears that will be shed – my own, as well as those of the many others who loved him. Tissues will be saturated, mascara will run, and chests will heave with sobs of grief.

It's appropriate to grieve, and it's perfectly reasonable to know it will happen. Yet tears and mourning are not the only things we can anticipate. While in the dark days that surround death, we may temporarily believe the sun will never shine again. It's hard to see in the darkness that life will go on, that the tears will one day end. But when they end, it is not just to give way to a dull, emotionless existence – not at all. Scripture tells us:

> *Those who sow in tears will reap with shouts of joy.*
> *Though one goes along weeping, carrying the bag of seed,*
> *he will surely come back with shouts of joy, carrying his*
> *sheaves.* (Psalm 126:5-6)

God's Word gives us this hope – that our tears will one day be replaced with shouts of joy. Therefore, we grieve today, but not as those who have no hope (1 Thessalonians 4:13). We cry today fully anticipating that one day we will again rejoice. Take heart.

DAY 154 – ATTENDED TO WITH LOVE

If Solomon was the wisest man who ever lived, Ethan the Ezrahite may have been a close second. Never heard of him? Me either! Yet in describing David's son, the writer of 1 Kings pointed out that Solomon was wiser than all other men, including Ethan the Ezrahite (1 Kings 4:31). So when Ethan speaks, people should listen!

And Ethan spoke, just once, as the author of Psalm 89, a song about the unwavering love of God. Surprisingly, at least to some of us, Ethan's song not only covered God's mighty power and continuous provision for Israel, but also mentioned God's correction.

As Dad, I always had difficulty convincing my girls that my correction was for their good and not an indication that I ceased to love them. They were kids, and let's face it, no correction at the time seems pleasant (Hebrews 12:11). God understands that, so as the loving Father He is, He had Ethan give us this reminder:

> *I will punish their sin with the rod, their iniquity with flogging; but I will not take my love from him, nor will I ever betray my faithfulness.* (Psalm 89:32-33)

We're tempted to see words like *punish, rod*, and *flogging* and think God's going to beat the tar out of us. But, *punish* here is a word that simply means *to visit or attend to*. If we step out of line, God will attend to that – He won't overlook it. He'll use whatever means necessary, sometimes just a gentle nudge to place us back on the right path. Other times, our greater stubbornness may lead to greater correction.

However, regardless of the means He uses to bring us back, He "attends to" us with an everlasting love. There will never, ever, ever be a time when He fails to love us or be faithful to us – even in the midst of our failures and times of being corrected.

Going through a time of discipline or other difficulty? Remember, He never withholds His love – ever!

DAY 155 – QUICK RESPONSE

*And a vision appeared to Paul in the night: a man of
Macedonia was standing there, urging him and saying,
"Come over to Macedonia and help us." And when Paul
had seen the vision, immediately we sought to go on into
Macedonia, concluding that God had called us to preach
the gospel to them.* (Act 16:9-10, ESV)

Paul and his team had wanted to take the Gospel to Asia Minor,
yet God's Spirit somehow prevented them from going there.
Through a dream, God impressed upon Paul the need to go to
Macedonia instead.

It's a passage which some folks make mystical by saying it's
"prescriptive" instead of "descriptive." In other words, because
God spoke through a dream once, that is His prescribed way of
speaking today. Personally, I believe this passage simply
describes what God did that night and is not to be taken as a
prescription that we should try to routinely fill today.

Instead of debating God's methods of communication, I'd like us
to focus on the response of Paul and his team. The new plan
didn't match their hopes. It didn't necessarily even make sense to
them. Yet look at how this group responded.

First, their response was immediate. They didn't debate it
amongst themselves or with God. Next, they eagerly sought to
go. Instead of looking for reasons not to proceed, they looked for
ways of making the new plan happen. Lastly, they considered the
matter settled. They concluded it was God's will, and they didn't
look back.

Regardless of how He speaks, how quick are you to obey the
clear command of God? Why might you hesitate? Give it some
thought.

DAY 156 – PROPPED UP OR THROWN DOWN?

We're "leaners." Each and every one of us leans upon something, or someone, during our times of trouble. Typically, our first inclination is to lean upon ourselves – our ability, our understanding, and our resources. Yet God's Word clearly tells us not to (Proverbs 3:5).

Once we come to an end of ourselves, many of us then turn to trusted friends or family. Certainly, we are to have them around during the hard times (Proverbs 27:10). However, Scripture is clear that eventually even our dearest friends and family can fail us (Job 19:14).

Ultimately, God wants us to fall upon Him. The same verse that tells us not to lean on our own understanding, first instructs us to *"Trust in the Lord with all our heart." Trust* in this verse comes from a word that means *to throw one down upon his face.* You see, we either try to prop ourselves up with shaky supports, or we throw ourselves down onto a rock-solid foundation which is God.

About these options, C.S. Lewis once wrote:

> *I see more clearly, I think, the necessity (if one may so put it) which God is under of allowing us to be afflicted – so few of us will really rest all on Him if He leaves us any other support.*

What do you do during your afflictions? Do you try to prop yourself up? Or do you throw yourself down upon the Lord? He wants us to rest fully in Him at all times – let's learn to throw ourselves on Him instead of leaning on shaky supports.

> *Trust in the Lord with all your heart and lean not on your own understanding…(Proverbs 3:5)*

DAY 157 – BEAUTIFUL INTENTIONS

When Job's three friends heard about all the troubles that had come upon him, they set out from their homes and met together by agreement to go and sympathize with him and comfort him. (Job 2:11)

Job's three friends (Eliphaz, Bildad, and Zophar) will end up getting a bad rap before their story is over, and understandably so. But, each time I read Job's account, I have to admit that I am initially very, very impressed with them. In fact, they model a great deal of behavior worth emulating.

We know very little about these guys other than the fact that when they heard their friend had suffered greatly, they agreed to gather together and go to him. They were willing to set aside their own lives – their families, their work, and their agendas – and make the journey to spend time with Job. Not only was their willingness commendable, so was their motivation.

As they set out from their homes and headed for the land of Uz, they went with the stated purposes of sympathizing with Job and bringing him comfort. What absolutely beautiful intentions. Scripture tells us that when they arrived and saw how severe Job's situation truly was, they mourned along with him and wept aloud.

If that were not amazing enough, what these men did next blew me away. For the next 7 days (and nights), they simply sat with Job in total silence. They practiced what I once heard called "the ministry of presence." They were just there with, and for, their friend.

In response to their friend's despair, these men went to bring sympathy and comfort, and they served him with their presence. All marks of a loving friendship. Are you willing to do likewise?

Joseph could have carried a massive chip on his shoulder. His brothers had sold him into slavery. His master's wife falsely accused him and he was thrown into prison without even so much as a trial. He was forgotten there for two years before being called upon to interpret Pharaoh's dream.

But God had plans for Joseph, and his shoulders weren't large enough to carry the burdens of Egypt AND a huge chip at the same time. So Joseph set aside his anger, bitterness, and thoughts of getting even. Instead, he moved forward with life. He got busy with his work, he married, and he became a father. In other words – he lived in the present, refusing to remain a prisoner of his past.

The degree of peace Joseph had come to reflected itself at the time of his first son's birth. When it came time to name the child, Joseph chose *Manasseh*. It's certainly not a name that has caught on in today's culture; however, it held deep, personal meaning for Joseph. For the name carried the meaning of *forgetting*, and Joseph selected it saying, "*It is because God has made me forget all my trouble and all my father's household.*" (Genesis 41:51)

Interestingly, the name of his second son, *Ephraim*, means *twice fruitful*, and Joseph chose it to remind himself that "*God has made me fruitful in the land of my suffering*" (41:52).

Mistreated and forced to suffer through no fault of his own, Joseph had two choices – become bitter and complain, or choose to forget the evils of the past and focus on the blessings of the present. He chose the path that led to joy; which are you choosing?

I'm rereading the account of Jacob and the family God chose to be His people. Honestly, they're messed up – which gives me hope! As many of you know, there were multiple wives involved, some favored, some not. The same thing happened with the children.

Through no fault of her own, Leah found herself married to a guy (Jacob) who preferred her sister (Rachel) and made no effort to conceal it. Conceiving and bearing children then became a twisted sort of competition between them – as I said, messed up.

But one of the wonderful things hidden in this sordid tale is the development within Leah. We see it in the names she chooses for her children. The name of the firstborn, Reuben (meaning *see, a son*), was selected because Leah believed God saw that she was hated and had rewarded her with a son to present to Jacob. Surely then he would love her. Likewise, Simeon (meaning *one who hears)* and Levi (meaning *attached*) were named in hopes that Jacob would finally attach himself to Leah.

It's all understandable if you're a spouse longing for love and attachment. But, for Leah love and connection would never come from Jacob. His heart always remained elsewhere. While bitterness was likely always near the door of her heart, I think the name Leah chose for her fourth son indicates that she found a way to rise above this bitterness and her disappointment. Listen to how Scripture records her next pregnancy: "'*This time I will praise the Lord.' Therefore she called his name Judah*" (Genesis 29:35).

Judah sounds like, and may be derived from, the Hebrew word for *praise*. And it is through the line of THAT child Christ would come.

Friends, when we spend the majority of our time seeking the approval and affection of others, we'll often be disappointed. But when we seek to praise God through our every action, He is pleased, and we will be satisfied.

Jimmy Durante, a great entertainer from years ago, was once asked to participate in a show for World War II veterans. His schedule was packed, but he told organizers he would do a short monologue if he could immediately leave for his next appointment. The organizers readily agreed, and Durante was booked.

When Durante took the stage, however, something changed. He went through the short skit as planned, but he didn't leave. The applause grew louder and louder, and Durante stayed and stayed. Before long, fifteen minutes had passed. Then twenty, then thirty.

Why do you think he stayed on stage? Perhaps, like me, you thought that once the spotlight came on and the crowd began to cheer, he just couldn't tear himself away. But let's read on.

At last Durante took his final bow. Backstage, someone said, "I thought you had to go after a few minutes? What happened?" Mr. Durante answered, "I did have to go, but I can show you the reason I stayed. You can see for yourself if you'll look down on the front row."

There, sitting side-by-side, were two veterans who had each lost an arm in the war. One had lost his right arm and the other his left arm. But together they were able to clap – and that's exactly what they were doing! The more they clapped, the longer Durante wanted to stay.

Pretty amazing picture, isn't it? Two "imperfect," "incomplete" people accomplishing together what they couldn't do alone. Friends, there's a reason God's Word tells us:

> *Though one may be overpowered, two can defend themselves. A cord of three strands is not quickly broken. (Ecclesiastes 4:12)*

We're not meant to do this Christian life alone. We need one another, and we can accomplish more by working together. With whom can you clap hands?

DAY 161 – THE HEART OF THE MATTER

Vision without action is only a dream. Action without vision just passes time. Vision with action can change the world.
-Joel A. Barker

Most people fall into one of two camps – they have visions of doing things but never get around to them, aka, the "dreamers." Or they maintain an extremely busy schedule filled with endless actions yet seem to lack real purpose, aka, the "aimless do'ers."

Sadly, it is perhaps in the frantic "doing" things that are relatively insignificant that we lose sight of the meaningful things we once desired. As Barker contends, however, if we can harness our actions to genuinely meaningful purposes – watch out, world!

For the follower of Christ, perhaps the best application of this concept is to harness our actions to the vision of Jesus. Since He told us His mission in life – "to seek and save the lost" (Luke 19:10) – doesn't it make sense for us to link our actions to that mission as well?

The wonderful thing is we can all do that in our own unique way. You don't have to quit your job and become a missionary. You don't have to sell your house and live among the homeless, or anything like that. What you may need to do, however, is begin looking for ways you can <u>harness your current life to the vision of Christ</u>. Begin asking, "How can I use my job to help Jesus seek and save the lost? How can I reach my unbelieving neighbors with the gospel? How could Jesus use my worldly possessions in His quest to save the souls of men?"

The "externals" may not need to change much, but the mindset and heart focus may. Give it some thought – how can you harness yourself to the mission of Christ, and thus avoid aimless activity?

> *For the Son of Man came to seek and to save the lost.*
> (Luke 19:10)

DAY 162 – WITNESSING HOPE

To be honest, I can hardly make myself watch the news anymore. The cruelty and senseless acts of violence are almost more than I can bear. Slowly and insidiously the events of this world chip away at an already fragile sense of hope which I cling to. When that happens, I need to ask myself in what (or whom) have I placed my hope.

Recently, I found an intriguing passage about hope that I hadn't noticed before. Listen to what the psalmist wrote about hope:

> *As for me, I will always have hope; I will praise You more and more. My mouth will tell of Your righteous deeds, of Your salvation all day long…* (Psalm 71:14-15)

If you ask me, stating that you'll always have hope sounds like a pretty bold claim. However, when we look at the writer's basis for that hope, it looks pretty solid. For this man's hope was not based on temporary things or upon himself. No, his hope was found in his praise of God's righteous deeds, his salvation that came from God, and his willingness to tell others about both. In essence, he found hope in telling others about the joy of salvation found only in God (Psalm 51:12).

Is hope a little hard to find these days? Consider being more deliberate in spending time praising God for who He is and telling others about what He's done.

DAY 163 – NINEVAH OR TARSHISH?

Like many of you, what I learned about Jonah as a child had more to do with a fish than it did a man. Rereading the story now, I recognize that the fish plays a minor part in the book, and the "main thing" deals with man and his obedience (or disobedience) to God.

The opening paragraph sets the stage. In it, we read that God told Jonah to go to Ninevah, and deliver a message of repentance. Jonah, however, having little love or regard for the 120,000 residents of the city, hightailed it as far from there as possible. So instead of heading 550 miles northeast by land to Ninevah, Jonah hopped a boat and sailed around 2500 miles in the opposite direction. In fact, in Jonah's day, Tarshish was the farthest extreme of the known world.

Interestingly, the same verse that says that Jonah zigged (to Tarshish) when God had said to zag (to Ninevah) adds this sad reality: "But Jonah rose to flee to Tarshish *from the presence of the Lord*" (Jonah 1:3, emphasis added). Sadly, Jonah's disobedience led him away from God.

If we're honest, the same choices and consequences exist for us today. Multiple times each day we will either obey God, or we'll disregard what He's told us. We answer His call or we refuse. And with each decision, we either move closer to Him or fall further away.

The choice is always ours – so choose Ninevah!

It's a remarkable example of authentic leadership. As they neared the Promised Land, God took Moses to the top of a mountain, from where he could see the land the Hebrews would soon possess. But Moses himself wouldn't set foot in the land because of his one moment of doubt and disobedience at Meribah.

There, Moses had struck a rock to get water to flow, instead of simply speaking to the rock. For that one act of disobedience, Moses wouldn't get to lead the people into their new homeland. But when God broke this news to Moses, Moses didn't complain to God; he didn't beg God to change his mind, as Moses had done on behalf of the Hebrews many times. No, when Moses heard the verdict, his reaction was this:

> *May the Lord, the God who gives breath to all living things, appoint someone over this community to go out and come in before them, one who will lead them out and bring them in, so the Lord's people will not be like sheep without a shepherd.* (Numbers 27:16-17)

Personally, I fear I may have had a few other thoughts to share with God! Thoughts like "That's not fair!" But Moses didn't say anything about himself, for his focus was on the people and what they'd need after he was gone. In my mind, THAT is leadership. While he lived, Moses constantly interceded for his people, and as he neared his end, Moses made provision for them after he was gone.

Where does such an "others focus" come from? Scripture tells us this about him: "*Now Moses was a very humble man, more humble than anyone else on the face of the earth*" (Number 12:3).

Humility allows us to place the needs of others above our own; it forms the roots from which authentic leadership can grow. Want to grow in leadership? Begin to think more frequently about meeting the needs of others.

DAY 165 – KINDLE FIRES

If the world seems cold to you, kindle fires to warm it.
-Lucy Larcom

If we're honest, this ol' world can seem cold and cruel much of the time. Life zooms by at a million miles per hour, and while there are endless social media options that are supposed to keep us connected, digital relationships are pretty cold and sterile. Sadly, even amidst hundreds or thousands of media "friends" we can often feel incredibly lonely and disconnected.

Over the last fifteen to twenty years, I believe the Facebook frenzy has encroached on the church. The desire and ability to actually engage with one another has suffered. Visitors to new churches may not be greeted because nobody within the building knows them, so they aren't extended a "Friend Request." They may leave feeling unnoticed, unwelcomed, and unwanted.

Even after joining a congregation, "breaking into the establishment" may be difficult. Perhaps you remember being the new kid on the block. Think back to what that was like and then make every effort to extend the right hand of fellowship to the newer members of your congregation (Galatians 2:9).

Lastly, if you're the new person having trouble getting established, may I suggest that you take Ms. Larcom's words to heart and kindle some fires until you sense the warmth of your new church family? Instead of waiting to be invited, invite. Instead of waiting to be welcomed, welcome. Instead of waiting for a hand to be extended to you, be the first to extend your hand to others. Should it be that way? I wish it weren't, but that may be the reality where we increasingly find ourselves living. Instead of giving UP on a church, first try giving OUT to them by kindling fires to warm it.

James, Cephas and John, those esteemed as pillars, gave me and Barnabas the right hand of fellowship when they recognized the grace given to me. (Galatians 2:9)

DAY 166 – ANALYSIS PARALYSIS

On the heels of a mighty victory over Canaan, the leaders of Israel (Deborah and Barak) sang a song which summarized each tribe's role in the big win. When it came to the tribe of Reuben, the lyric was this:

> *In the districts of Reuben there was much searching of heart. Why did you stay among the sheep pens to hear the whistling for the flocks? In the districts of Reuben there was much searching of heart.* (Judges 5:15-16)

While it's not readily apparent in the English translation, the idea behind the verses above is that Reuben continuously pondered the wisdom of joining the battle. At first they had the resolve to answer God's call to join in the fight, but then they debated (within their tribe) the wisdom of such actions. "Should we or shouldn't we?"

Back and forth the self-talk went until in the end…they did nothing! Instead of answering God's call to join Him in His fight, Reuben was lulled to sleep by their comfort. As one commentator put it, Reuben made great promises, "…but they only ended in sloth and vacillation. They decided to go, and—stayed at home."

Sadly, I'm far too familiar with this sort of "analysis paralysis." Frequently my initial resolve gets trumped by my "searching of heart." I begin to doubt the wisdom of acting – after all, I'm pretty comfortable "as is." Sometimes that may be okay. However in situations like Reuben's, the call is directly from God, and getting paralyzed by our ponderings is simply disobedience wrapped up in over-thinking. That moment of certainty may never arrive; make the best decision you can with the information available at the time, trust God, and move on!

Has God called you to do something on His behalf? Don't overthink it; follow through on your initial resolve before your courage fades away.

DAY 167 – SAFE IN THE HARBOR

Yesterday, we looked at how the tribe of Reuben failed to answer God's call to action due to their overanalyzing. Today, we'll look at another reason we may not respond to God's call – fear.

In the song of praise Deborah sang following Israel's victory over Canaan, the verse about the tribe of Asher said this:

> *Asher remained at the seashore and stayed in his harbors.*
> (Judges 5:17, HCSB)

Asher's territory was on the shores of the Mediterranean, and they were one of the greatest maritime nations of the world at that time. They had great ships which could have contributed significantly to Israel's cause against Canaan. Could have…but didn't.

Instead, those ships remained in Asher's harbors. *Remained* in this verse literally means *sat*. Asher simply sat where they were, immobilized by fear. In my childhood home there was a poster which read, "A ship in the harbor is safe, but that is not what a ship is built for." I wish I could say that truth always inspired me to set sail on the open seas of life.

Yet far too often, I have chosen the safety of the harbor over an adventure at sea with God. Like Asher, I stay put – paralyzed by fear. I risk nothing, so I lose nothing – or so I tell myself. But by choosing the harbor, we may miss our destiny. We lose out on the opportunity to trust God. We lose out on the opportunity to experience victory in Him.

A harbor is the place where ships are supposed to dock only long enough to be restocked and/or repaired. Nobody ever built a boat only to see it sit in the harbor. Likewise, God didn't create you to sit safely by the dock – He created you to sail with Him. Will you untie the rope?

DAY 168 – ONE OF THESE THINGS…

The fruit of the Spirit is love, joy, peace, PRIDE, kindness….

Okay, stop the presses and cue the old Sesame Street, "One of these things doesn't belong here" music….

I'm sad to say that recently, I let pride take the place of patience in a conversation – and would you believe it didn't go very well for anyone involved? At such times, I really wish I had a DVR (Dave Vitt Recorder) that could stop life and allow me to rewind and have a "do-over." As we all know, however, life has no rewind button, and there are no do-overs.

Scripture says that pride and destruction are the best of friends – they are never very far apart. I'd always thought of that verse (Proverbs 16:18) in terms of the harm one brings upon themselves as a result of their pride. And certainly, many times the destruction we cause is our own. However, I have witnessed firsthand that sometimes our pride destroys others – often those we care about the most.

The best option is obviously to "get it right" the first time, to let His Spirit govern every thought, every action, every word. But unfortunately, that is not reality for any of us. Thankfully, for those times when we've blown it, there is a precious gift called forgiveness. Once sought, and granted, it will not bring a do-over but does allow for second and third (and seventy-times-seven) chances.

DAY 169 – GLORIFYING WORK

It was the night of the last supper, and in what has come to be known as the "Upper Room Discourse," Jesus spent those last few hours teaching His disciples some final, important lessons.

Near the end of their time together, Jesus said something that really jumped off the page:

> *"I glorified You on earth, <u>having accomplished the work that You gave Me</u> to do"* (John 17:4, emphasis added)

In Christ's case, the work the Father gave was leaving His throne in heaven and laying down His life as the perfect sacrifice for the sins of the world. The result not only made heaven accessible for mankind, but also glorified the Father in the process.

Friends, God has work for us to do while we're here too. Some types of God-given work that leap to mind are loving one another, sharing the gospel, making disciples, and giving to those in need. The specifics of how we fulfill those instructions vary for each of us – your sphere of influence is different from everyone else's. However, the outcome is the same – we bring glory to God when we do His work.

Jesus not only set the example by His own life, He also passed the command on to us – "Let your light shine before men in such a way that they may see your good works, and glorify your Father who is in heaven" (Matthew 5:16).

One last thought. Jesus did not need to work in order to earn His Father's love or acceptance – He worked to glorify His Daddy. The same is true for us as well. As children of God, we don't work to earn His love; we live to bring Him glory.

DAY 170 – I FORGOT!

Each year CareerBuilders.com conducts a survey of nearly 5000 managers and employees to collect some of the more "creative" excuses given for missed days of work. Some of my favorites included:

- Employee couldn't come to work because she accidentally got on an airplane!
- Employee claimed the ozone in the air flattened his tires!
- Employee woke up in a good mood and didn't want to ruin it!
- Employee was too upset after watching *The Hunger Games*!

But I think this was my favorite – Employee didn't show up because he forgot he'd been hired for the job! Pretty funny stuff (unless you're their employers).

Yet I wonder if we don't make similar excuses for not completing the work God has assigned to us. Various distractions are like "planes" we accidentally get on. Over-committing our time often leaves us with "flat" emotional "tires." Or perhaps we allow our mood to dictate if we'll serve or not. Sadly, it's even possible that we can completely forget that God has "hired us" for a job at all.

Yes, our salvation is a free gift from God through faith in Christ. But from the moment we accept Him as Savior, He is also to become Lord (aka Master). In practical terms, we no longer live for ourselves or call all the shots. As Scripture says, "*You are not your own. You were bought at a price*" (1 Corinthians 6:19-20).

God has created each of His children to serve Him in some manner. But the question remains – will we show up for the job, or will we find reasons not to? Faithful service to your God just may be the missing link to your satisfaction; why not give it a try?

DAY 171 – NO JOKE

But his sons-in-law thought he was joking. (Genesis 19:14)

What a tragic statement. There had been nothing funny about what Lot had said, and there was absolutely nothing to laugh about afterward either.

An angel had told Lot what God was about to do. In his mercy, God gave Lot the chance to warn his family and enough time for all to escape. Yet the young men found the idea of judgment from God so laughable they chose to ignore the warnings. Sadly, Lot left with his wife and two daughters only. The sons-in-law, ignoring the warnings of God, were never heard from again.

Unfortunately, these men weren't the first to misjudge God's settled opposition to sin, and they certainly weren't the last. So many people today think that God is only love; they ignore the equally-true aspect of God that balances that love – His absolute justice. God is so serious about sin that He sacrificed His own Son to pay its penalty. Folks, that's no laughing matter.

Sin and a coming judgment are still relevant today. In the New Testament we read, *"people are destined to die once, and after that to face judgment"* (Hebrews 9:27). All die. All face judgment thereafter. No joke.

Thankfully, the very next verse tells us, *"Christ was sacrificed once to take away the sins of many; and He will appear a second time, not to bear sin, but to bring salvation to those who are waiting for him"* (v.28).

Lot's sons-in-law were given a choice, and so are we. I'm guessing those men wish they'd chosen differently. We should learn from them and chose Christ while we can. And as we're able, let's encourage others to do so too.

DAY 172 – BEGINNING A NEW CYCLE

Although God referred to him as a "mighty warrior," he's most frequently remembered for his "rash vow" (a promise that cost him his daughter; Judges 11:31-35).

The man I'm referring to is Jephthah – a guy who overcame incredible odds to lead Israel for six years as their judge. But his story started much differently. Scripture introduces him this way:

> *Jephthah the Gileadite was a mighty warrior. His father was Gilead; his mother was a prostitute.* (11:1)

There it is, for the whole world to see – the son of a prostitute. While this is still stigmatized today, in ancient Israel the shame was much greater. So much so that Jephthah's brothers (the sons of Gilead's actual wife) drove him away. They refused to count him among their number; they denied him any inheritance as a brother.

Yet what they discarded into the trash heap, God recycled and used in a mighty way! As it turned out, when the Ammonites attacked Israel, the Hebrews had nobody to defend them. So whom did they call? None other than Jephthah. And despite being grossly mistreated by his countrymen earlier, Jephthah answered the call and successfully defeated Ammon.

It's an amazing story filled with hope for those born into difficult circumstances. You see, within one generation, Jephthah was able to overcome the obstacle of family shame. The same is true for you and I today as well. With God's help we are NOT destined to continue destructive, shameful family cycles.

Friends, all families have a generational cycle – if yours is a great one, thank God and do your best to maintain it. However, if it's been a destructive one, ask God to help you begin a new cycle today. It only takes one child to stand up and say, "Enough! I'm going to take my family down a different path!" With His help you CAN do it – in one generation!

DAY 173 – IF ONLY…

He may not have known it at the time, but as he wrestled with his losses and the accusations of his friends, Job uttered one of the greatest needs man has ever known.

At the end of the ninth chapter, after a few rounds of point and counterpoint with his friends, Job pleaded for the chance to take his case directly to God. He was utterly weary of defending his innocence before his friends and welcomed the opportunity to have God hear him.

That was Job's wish, yet it presented a problem for him. While he was innocent of the wrongdoing of which his friends accused him, Job knew he was not holy enough to stand before a perfect and righteous God. So, Job felt hopelessly stuck between his wrongly judging friends, and THE perfect Judge.

It was in that desperation that Job said these words:

> *He is not a mere mortal like me that I might answer Him, that we might confront each other in court. If only there were someone to mediate between us, someone to bring us together, someone to remove God's rod from me, so that His terror would frighten me no more. Then I would speak up without fear of Him, but as it now stands with me, I cannot. (Job 9:32-35).*

"If only there were someone to mediate between us…" There is, Job, there is! Jesus perfectly fit the job description Job painted. Christ mediates between the Father and us (1 John 2:1), He reconciles men to God (Romans 5:10), He removes God's punishment (Hebrews 2:7), and through Him we are granted access to the Father (Ephesians 2:8).

Today, give thanks that, in Christ, we have an Advocate with the Father.

DAY 174 – DOOR PRIZES

Imagine the following ad appeared in your local paper.

<u>Attention</u>: *A meeting will be held this Thursday night for all those who are needy, hurting, humble, hungry, disappointed, persecuted, self-denying, misunderstood, falsely-accused, slandered, and insulted. All are welcome.*

Would you respond? Or have you concluded that folks like the ones above are to be avoided? We spend most of our lives trying to promote ourselves, and in the process we attempt to hide any shred of evidence that we are less than perfect. But here's the beauty of God's system as compared to man's…<u>What the world chooses to discard as worthless, God chooses to bless and use.</u>

Check out what those who attended the meeting received as door prizes (and what you and I may have missed if we didn't want to associate with that crowd):

> *Blessed are the poor in spirit, for theirs is the kingdom of heaven. Blessed are those who mourn, for they will be comforted. Blessed are the meek, for they will inherit the earth. Blessed are those who hunger and thirst for righteousness, for they will be filled. Blessed are the merciful, for they will be shown mercy. Blessed are the pure in heart, for they will see God. Blessed are the peacemakers, for they will be called sons of God. Blessed are those who are persecuted because of righteousness, for theirs is the kingdom of heaven. Blessed are you when people insult you, persecute you and falsely say all kinds of evil against you because of me. Rejoice and be glad, because great is your reward in heaven. (Matthew 5:3-12)*

What do they receive? Oh, just comfort, an inheritance, satisfaction, mercy, God Himself, and an eternal reward. Maybe I'll recheck my calendar for Thursday night! How about you?

DAY 175 – BETTER?

Wouldn't it be better for us to go back…? (Numbers 14:3)

In this case, those words were uttered by the Israelites upon hearing that the land they had been promised to inhabit was filled with enemies- enemies who were both numerous and gigantic! The majority report from the twelve spies was that the odds of defeating the Canaanites were minimal, or worse, it just couldn't be done.

So when the going got tough, the majority got out the white flag and said, "Wouldn't it just be better if we gave up and went back to where we came from?" We shake our heads at them because we know the outcome. We know that God intervened and won the day. We know that the giants in the land were no match for the God of angel armies (1 Samuel 17). We know, and perhaps they should have known too.

But, if we're honest, we also know that bumping up against the hard stuff of life chips away at our faith. When the obstacles become numerous and large, the temptation is to become discouraged and think it's too difficult to proceed. So we wonder what the Israelites wondered – would it be better just to go back?

I understand the pull of discouragement; I get the tug of defeat. I'm as prone as anyone to look at an uncertain future with its unknown threats and conclude that the better choice is the known past – even if that past was less than ideal. It was at least familiar.

Friends, the answer to Israel's question was a resounding "NO!" Back to slavery in Egypt under cruel taskmasters was NOT better. Similarly, the answer when we're tempted to retreat from advancements God intends to use to expand our faith should also be a thundering "NO!" God wants us to walk forward with Him in faith. Will we?

When Moses came down from Mount Sinai with the two tablets of the covenant law in his hands, he was not aware that his face was radiant because he had spoken with the LORD. (Exodus 34:29)

When I was young, this verse made me think of the "glow-in-the-dark" trinkets that used to come in "Specially Marked Boxes" of some cereals. After being held close to a light, they would shine in the dark for a while. I guess I pictured Moses having that type of glow after he had spent time near the Light of the world.

Moses's appearance was so radically changed that he had to cover his face when interacting with others (verse 33). One thing is for sure – others KNEW Moses had spent time with God. And folks, the same should be true for us as well!

No, I'm not suggesting that we'll begin to glow like the Swamp Thing from an episode of *Scooby Doo*, but the fact that we spend time with the God of the Universe should become readily apparent to others. Our speech and action should differ, and the desires of our heart should change. To look at it from the other side of the coin, if we remain exactly as we've always been, why is God making no difference in our lives?

As one innocent child observed on the way home from church, "Mom, if God is so big that He holds the entire universe in His hand, and yet lives inside us when we accept Jesus – shouldn't He shine through?"

Friends, if you and I spend meaningful time with the God of the universe, He will shine through. Is He?

DAY 177 – GIVEN THE CHANCE

Lost amidst the horrifying news of the day was an overlooked report that deserves our attention. According to several news outlets, a study of young adults (aged eighteen to twenty-nine) in the UK revealed that an overwhelming 89 percent felt their lives were "meaningless and without purpose." (Up from ten percent only ten years earlier).

Other findings indicated that 30 percent were "stuck in a rut," and 84 percent acknowledged that they were failing to "live their best life." Sadly, the majority of participants (51 percent) believed the primary reason humanity was placed on earth was to be happy.

With religion being a major source of sense of purpose, a separate survey reported last month that those professing a Christian faith in the UK is at a record low of 38 percent, with only one percent of eighteen to twenty-four year-olds identifying as belonging to the Church of England.

Is there a correlation? I'll allow you to draw your own conclusions. One more observation from the original UK study – "More than a third of Brits would completely start their lives over given the chance."

Friends, here is the good news of the gospel – YOU CAN!!! You've been given the chance to start life over! Jesus called it being "born again" (John 3:3,7). In fact, Christ claimed that is the only way to enter heaven or meet the Father – where real meaning and purpose are found.

Finding life meaningless and without purpose? Hit the Reset button that only Christ offers!

> *Jesus replied, "Very truly I tell you, no one can see the kingdom of God unless they are born again." (John 3:3)*

DAY 178 – EK OR EIS?

The words look and sound so much alike, but, oh, what a difference a few letters make.

Exegesis is *the critical evaluation and interpretation of a text.* It is derived from *EK*, a Greek preposition meaning *out of*, with the rest of the word being related to *leading or guidance*. So in exegesis, we're essentially attempting to evaluate and interpret the text in such a way as to get the correct meaning **out of** what the author has written.

Eisegesis is that similar-looking and -sounding word that means something completely different, however. In Greek, *EIS* is a preposition that means *into*, so as Webster's states, eisegesis is *the interpretation of a text (such as of the Bible) by **reading into** it one's own ideas.* Instead of allowing Scripture to guide and lead us, we begin with our own thoughts and ideas, and allow those to define the meaning of Scripture.

If we're honest, it's tempting to "EIS" instead of "EK." Often we want Scripture to mean what we WANT it to mean rather than what's actually written. Or we may read the Bible through the lenses of our own experience. However, unless we approach Scripture with a sincere effort to determine what the text meant to the original readers, we have little chance of seeing what it means to us today. As Gordon Fee and Douglas Stuart note in their book, *How to Read the Bible for all It's Worth,* "A text cannot mean (today) what it never meant (originally)."

Only after we've determined what was meant then, can we begin to ask ourselves what it means for us today. What it meant then and what it means today – both are essential to the correct understanding and application of God's Word.

As we open His Word, let's remember to let Him do the talking!

DAY 179 – ALL OUR DAYS

I recently ran across a verse that I believe to be true, but I have yet to fully incorporate it into my life as if it is true. You see, if I genuinely lived as if it were true, I'd approach life with more security and less fear. What verse am I referring to?

> *All the days ordained for me were written in Your book before one of them came to be.* (Psalm 139:16)

What does it mean that God *ordained* all David's days? The original word was used to describe a potter working with clay, or a carver working with wood. The idea is that God *formed* the days, *planned* the days, and *determined their purpose*. Perhaps most importantly, God had such purpose and plans for ALL of David's days. And since God is sovereign, His oversight over individual lives continues today.

To accept these words at face value means that we accept that God fully controls each and every day we will ever see. There is nothing that we can do to eke out any additional days, and there is nothing we can do to lessen those days. How that works in concert with our free will remains a puzzle to me, but we can still trust that He has all the plans for us and all the purposes under control. We need not fear that God will fail to fulfill His plan through us, and that means our days are all His.

DAY 180 – THE SEVENTH

It's not here yet, but it's coming.

King David must have been looking out from his palace window as he wrote Psalm 144. Of this Psalm, Charles Spurgeon once wrote:

> A Psalm of David. No doubt written after some great victory, and also before another severe struggle. The Christian man seldom escapes from one difficulty without falling into another. Thanks be unto God, He that is with us in six troubles will not forsake us in the seventh!

Yes, we can (and should) be glad that the God who has seen us through six battles will be with us as we come to the seventh. None of us want to face that next struggle without Him. But, if we're honest, we look forward to the day when that next battle just never arrives, because peace arrives instead.

David foresaw that day. As he brought his song to an end, he sang, "*There will be no breaching of walls, no going into captivity, no cry of distress in our streets. Blessed is the people of whom this is true; blessed is the people whose God is the Lord*" (verses 14-15).

In other words, for the genuine children of God, the day is coming when the last struggle will be forever behind us. John stated it this way: "*He will wipe every tear from their eyes. There will be no more death, or mourning or crying or pain, for the old order of things has passed away*" (Revelation 21:4).

It's not here yet, but it's coming! Until that day, thank God that He will not forsake you in your seventh battle.

ABOUT THE AUTHOR

Author, teacher, pharmacist, business owner, dad, husband, and life-long student…each role has helped shape the man, as well as the book you're holding. While Dave has a Master's Degree in Christian Counseling, plus additional seminary training, he lives in the real world, having worked as a pharmacist and owned his own business for many years. In addition, Dave has been married for over thirty-two years and has raised two beautiful adult daughters. Therefore, he brings a very real, sometimes raw, but always practical, perspective to his teaching. His previous works include, *Volumes 1, 2 and 3 of The Teachable Heart Devotional Series,* and *James – Living a Life of Faith: A Bible Study for Men.*

Dave has taught adult Bible study classes for more than twenty years and considers it among the greatest joys of life. Today, he lives in suburban Kansas City with his wife and daughter. Wherever a group of Teachable Hearts gathers, he humbly looks forward to teaching.